I0559668

Rewriting the Script

The Power of Transforming Inner Dialogue in
Oppressed Communities

By
**Mardoche Sidor, MD, Adaiah Lassalle, LCSW,
Karen Dubin, PhD, LCSW, the SWEET Institute**

SWEET Institute Publishing
Transformational Books for a Transformational World

Published by:
SWEET Institute Publishing
New York, NY

First Edition
Printed in the United States of America

ISBN (Paperback): 978-1-968105-10-5
Library of Congress Control Number: 2025943859

Cover Design by SWEET Institute Publishing
Interior Design and Layout by SWEET Institute Publishing

For bulk orders, permissions, or media inquiries, please contact:
contact@sweetinstitute.com

Unless otherwise noted, all stories and case examples in this book are either fictionalized or used with permission, and identifying details have been changed to protect the privacy of individuals.

SWEET Institute Publishing
Transformational Books for a Transformational World

Dedication

For every soul who has ever doubted their worth because of someone else's words.

For those who carry invisible wounds, and for those who dared to begin healing.

For our ancestors, whose survival made our freedom possible.

For the next generation—may you inherit new stories, new voices, and a world brave enough to honor your truth.

And for all who choose, every day, to rewrite the script—
this book is for you.

Other Books by Mardoche Sidor, M.D; Karen Dubin, PhD, LCSW; with the SWEET Institute

- Journey to Empowerment
- Discovering Your Worth: Everything You Need to Feel Fulfilled
- The Power of Faith: A Harvard-Trained Psychiatrist Speaking on Faith
- The Psychotherapy Certificate Course: The Clinician and Coach Manual (Books 1–3)
- The Anxiety Course: The Workbook
- What's Missing
- NLP for Clinicians
- 50 SWEET Poems: Reflections on life, love and self
- The Power of Belief: How Ideas Shape Leaders, Nations and the Future
- The Courage to Care: Stories of Healing, Hope, and the Power of Social Work: Told by   Over 50 SWEET Institute Social Workers
- Transforming Team Relationships from the Inside Out: The SWEET Healing Circle for Agencies: Redefining Accountability, Collaboration, and Culture
- Remembering: The Journey Back to the Pre-Conditioned Self
- The Clinician's Mirror: A Story of Projection, Self-Awareness, and Transformation for Clinicians
- The Secret Is in Remembering: Why We Suffer, Why We Forget, and How to Return to Who We Are
- It's All Perfect: What If Nothing in Your Life Was a Mistake?
- Because of Us: Why Outcomes Change When We Do
- Before Anything Else, Validate: The Missing Link in Healing, Leadership, Relationships, and Personal Growth

Table of Contents

Foreword

By Donna Sue Johnson, LCSW
Social Worker, Clinician, and Advocate for Over 40 Years
Specialist in HIV/AIDS, Mental Illness, Addiction, and LGBTQ+
Elders
Member of SAGE and GRIOT Circle

I have spent over four decades walking alongside people on the margins—those whose voices were silenced, whose bodies were pathologized, whose stories were overlooked, and whose identities were questioned or erased. I have held hands with individuals battling HIV/AIDS in the early years of the epidemic, listened to the unheard pain of those struggling with addiction and mental illness, and sat in circle with LGBTQ+ elders whose wisdom has too often gone unrecognized.

And over all these years, I've learned something that no textbook ever taught me:
What breaks people is not just what happens to them; rather, it's what they come to believe about themselves because of it. That is internalized oppression.
It is subtle, it is insidious, and it is everywhere.

I see it in the man who won't apply for housing because he's sure he'll be turned down. I see it In the woman who apologizes for taking up space in a waiting room; and I see it in the elder who shrinks their voice in meetings even though their life experience could light the room.

These are not isolated behaviors. These are symptoms of a larger disease—a disease of the mind and spirit, born from centuries of injustice, stigma, and systemic exclusion. This is exactly why Rewriting the Script is not just a book—it's a balm, a blueprint, and a breakthrough.

This work does what so few books dare to do: It walks alongside the people, without judgment.

It validates the silent battles happening inside our own minds. It offers tools not only to understand the pain, but to change the pattern.

I especially love that this book does not view healing as a solo journey. It reminds us that healing is relational, cultural, and collective. The authors bring together clinical wisdom, spiritual depth, and community care in a way that makes liberation not just a concept— but a daily practice. And as someone who believes in holistic care— body, mind, heart, and spirit—this book feels like home to me.

Whether you're a clinician, a caregiver, a perseverer, a leader, or simply someone trying to heal and grow—this book will walk with you, it will challenge you, it will soften you, and it will strengthen you. Most importantly, it will remind you that you are not alone—and that your liberation is not only possible, but contagious.

Let this book be a mirror, a map, and a message to your soul:

You are not broken.
You are not too late.
And you are absolutely enough.

With deep love and respect,
Donna Sue Johnson, LCSW

Preface

By Anne Elizabeth Straub, LCSW-R
Social Worker, Clinician, and Advocate for Over 40 Years, Mentor, Health Consultant
Social Justice and Environmental Activist
SWEET Member and Experiential Learning Leader and Community Healer
National Multiple Sclerosis Society Partner in Care
Chair, Social Workers Advancing Human Animal Bond (SWAHAB)

Not all pain shows up on diagnostic checklists, lab work, MRI's or X-rays.
It doesn't always have a name, but it makes its presence known. You feel it in the way you silence yourself in a meeting, in the hesitation before you speak your truth, in the quiet shame that flares when you try to take up space., and in the belief that perhaps—just maybe—you are not enough.

This book gives language to that pain. It calls it what it is: internalized oppression. It offers something few books dare to provide: not only a path toward understanding it, but a way to rewrite the story.

I have spent over four decades walking beside people as they navigate the challenges of trauma, disability, grief, systemic injustice, and loss of voice and navigated much of that territory in my own life, dealing chronic pain, chronic illness and disability.

As a clinician, mentor, advocate, and someone who has sat in the circle of the SWEET Institute since its beginning, I know that healing requires more than information—it requires transformation. It requires community. It requires a shift from knowing to doing, from surviving to liberating.

Throughout my years immersed in SWEET, I have seen what happens when clinicians reclaim their own narratives. They become more effective, and their lives improve. They grow in new and unexpected ways. They hold space in a way that liberates, rather than replicates, oppression. This book brings that possibility to life—for everyone.

Rewriting the Script embodies all of this.

This book is not theoretical. It is experiential. It reflects the kind of learning and implementation that changes lives. Its pages invite the reader—whether clinician, educator, caregiver, organizer, or seeker—to pause, to reflect, to name what was never truly theirs, and to choose a new voice.

It is not meant to be read passively. Enter it. You will be challenged, affirmed, and gently guided toward the part of yourself that already knows:
You were never the problem. You were simply living inside a script that was never yours.
This book reminds us that healing is not about perfection—it's about return, a return to voice, a return to truth, a return to self.

Let it guide you there, and let it remind you that you belong in the story you are now rewriting.

Anne Elizabeth Straub, LCSW-R,
Social Worker, Clinician, and Advocate for Over 40 Years

Introduction — Breaking the Silence on Inner Dialogue and Oppression

Why This Book Matters, and Why It's Yours Now

By Adaiah Lassalle, LCSW

Black Woman, Social Worker, Healer, and Co-Author

Most people think of oppression as an external force. It is oversimplified as being based on race, one's sex or socioeconomic class while neglecting its presence in many other "isms" based on ability, sexual orientation, physical appearance, and ethnocentrism to name a few. It's impact only being reflected in systems, policies, institutions, stereotypes, and profiling with law enforcement. They think of oppression as something historical, in workplace dynamics, housing, wealth and health care. However, oppression does not only exist externally but internally as well. It becomes a voice in our head. It becomes a voice that says" I'm not good enough," "I'm not worth as much", "I have to work twice as hard or be twice as good to be recognized and secure in my position". It permeates our beliefs about ourselves, others, and our communities.

These inner narratives have a source. They are inherited, strengthened, and practiced so often that we believe they are our own, that they define who or what we are allowed to be. We are told it is a deflated sense of self, self-doubt, or insecurity when in fact, it is something that can be more sinister, commanding and restraining. It is our inner dialogue that has been colonized and forged by oppression.

Rewriting the script has resonated with me as both a Black Full-Figured Woman and a clinician and social worker. I have experienced the intersectionality of oppression in the forms of racism, sexism, classism, and weight stigma. My experiences were validated by terms like the "Black Tax" that highlights the financial, social, emotional, and psychological challenges stemming from systemic and institutional racism and discrimination. Alice Walker's term "womanist" that highlights the influence of sexism, racism and classism play in Black Women's experiences. And weight stigma referring to the devaluation, denigration and oppression experienced because of being overweight and my physical appearance. All of these "isms" impacted by internal dialogue, my relationship with myself and others, my career path, finances, and contribution.

As a social worker, and clinician, I have seen the damage silence and unfamiliarity about internalized oppression can cause. I have worked with brilliant, perseverant and empowering people of color, LGBTQ+ youth, women navigating sexist expectations, elders who have carried decades of stigma and are now facing ageism, people dealing with physical and mental disabilities, who all shared one thing in common: They have been taught to second guess their own voice and doubt their self-worth and contribution.

Re-writing the Script has increased my awareness of not only externalized oppression and my internalized oppressor; but also provided a pathway to healing, an opportunity to transform and evolve by addressing the root causes. This book stemmed from the realization that liberation is an internal process that is shaped by the belief that healing is to be shared-across generations, communities, and across every barrier that once told us to stay quiet, to avoid, to accept or surrender.

Why Now?

We are living through a time when systemic injustice, collective trauma, hidden truths, and deep inequities are becoming harder to deny or justify. They detract from our sense of wholeness and oneness as human beings. Yet, the most dangerous consequence of oppression is still the one we don't see-the one that dwells and flourishes inside that lives in our internal dialogue, in our thoughts, feelings, beliefs, behaviors, perceptions, and in the meaning we assign to ourselves, others and the world. While protests, changing policies, uncovering historical truths and awareness of these issues are all vital, we also must oppose and dispute the internalized voice. We must dispute that voice that tells us, "We don't deserve to be here, we are inadequate or too much, we should be self-sacrificing and humble." We must dispute the voice that tells us that "we are not as intelligent, and our bodies must adhere to a specific set of social constructs of beauty.

This book delivers psychoeducation about historical trauma, generational wounds and the ramifications of inherited and propagated shame, fear, and limitation. It provides information about the neuroscience of marginalization and internalized stress while highlighting how we respond and how this response serves to support or hinder our journey of self-discovery and empowerment. You will become aware of the voice of the inner oppressor, and you will learn to notice, name and navigate it. You will learn to exchange it with language rooted in respect, truth, and power. This roadmap utilizes journaling, self-affirming statements, guided reflections, and additional resources that will serve as both your liberation kit and inspire change and the power to transform our thoughts and beliefs about ourselves and what we can accomplish. Lastly, it offers insight into how our personal healing can stimulate change in our family, communities, and society in general. In sum, it will offer you a path that is compassionate, empowering, creative, and practical for re-writing the script that was never truly yours.

Let us begin together, in truth, oneness, courage and in love to navigate the passageway of self-liberation and freedom.

Adaiah Lassalle, LCSW

Introduction — Why This Book Matters

By Karen Dubin, Ph.D., LCSW

Woman. Social Worker. Clinician. Educator. Healer. Co-Author.

We are often told to work on ourselves — to be more confident, more positive, more resilient.

We're encouraged to practice self-care, use affirmations, build self-esteem; yet, most of these strategies skim the surface. They tell us to heal ourselves without ever acknowledging the deeper truth: That our inner world has been shaped by outer forces designed to keep us small. That's why healing our inner dialogue is not optional. It's essential.

Inner dialogue shapes everything: How we see ourselves, how we treat ourselves, what we believe is possible, and how we show up in relationships, in our work, in our leadership. Inner dialogue is essential because most of all it shapes how we carry or challenge the systems we've internalized.

As a woman and a social worker, I've sat across from countless individuals who, regardless of age or background, carried this same invisible burden: The harshness in their voice, the shame in their silence, and the fear of being "too much" or "not enough." I've witnessed brilliant, beautiful people shrink before their own thoughts. I've felt it in myself, too.

We cannot dismantle systems of oppression while still obeying the voices they planted inside us. This book matters because it helps us finally hear that voice — and gives us a path to transform it.

Inner Dialogue Shapes Identity Inner dialogue is not just what we mutter to ourselves at the end of a long day; rather, it's the constant narration that informs how we love, how we speak, how we dream. It shapes how we ask for help, how we set boundaries, and how we see our worth. And when that voice has been shaped by sexism, racism, colonization, classism, ableism, and other systems of harm, it becomes a distorted script we carry — silently, obediently, often unknowingly.

And because it's quiet, it rarely gets challenged. And because it's familiar, we often mistake it for truth. This book invites you to pause — to listen, and to unlearn, to interrupt the lies that have been living in our mind — and begin to rewrite the truth.

How Oppression Rewrites the Mind

Oppression is not only political or structural. It's psychological. It shapes how we think, how we feel, and how we exist in our own skin. It teaches us to over-function and under-receive, to question our intuition, to prove our worth through exhaustion, and to distrust ease, softness, and joy. It also teaches us that our authentic self is not welcome — or not enough.

Once again, these internalized scripts are not just painful. They are passed on. to our children, to our clients, to our students, and to ourselves — over and over again.
Even when the oppressive systems are no longer in the room, the voice they implanted often still is. This book is here to help you change that.

The Goal of This Book

This book is not a lecture; rather, it's a healing circle, a space of unlearning, a mirror, a guide, and a reclamation.

The goal is not perfection — it's liberation. The goal is not a new mask of positivity — it's a deeper, truer voice rooted in dignity, clarity, and love. The goal is not to fix you — because you were never broken; rather, the goal is to return you to yourself.

You will be gently, honestly, step-by-step, guided to:
- Hear the voice you've been living with
- Understand where it came from
- Interrupt it without shame
- Replace it with language that affirms your truth and humanity
- Practice a new way of speaking to yourself
- Pass on this new narrative to your clients, your communities, your children, your world

The revolution begins within. But it doesn't end there; rather, it echoes, it ripples, and it liberates.

This is not just a book to read; rather, it's a book to live, to return to, to share, and to embody.

Let's begin.

— Karen Dubin, Ph.D., LCSW

What This Book Is About

This is not just a book about psychology. It is not just a book about oppression. It is a book about the intersection between the two — and what happens when we finally name what's been happening inside us all along.

Rewriting the Script is about healing the voice in your head that was never truly yours. It is about how systems of racism, sexism, colonization, classism, ableism, ageism, homophobia, transphobia, and other forms of structural violence have shaped our internal narratives — and how we begin to reclaim them. It's about the painful truth that many of the thoughts we live with daily are not evidence of personal failure, rather, the predictable result of systems that taught us to doubt ourselves.

This book is about ending that inheritance.

It offers a clear, step-by-step path to:

- Recognize internalized oppression for what it is
- Hear your inner dialogue with new awareness
- Interrupt the inner critic without shame
- Replace those narratives with truth, dignity, and compassion
- Make this healing sustainable through daily practice
- And ripple it outward — into families, communities, and systems

You will walk with us through four transformative parts:

1. Understanding the Origins — How oppressive systems shape the inner critic
2. Exploring the Psychology of Liberation — How internalized oppression warps identity, safety, and relationships
3. Applying Tools for Inner Liberation — Awareness, Disruption, Replacement, Repetition
4. Moving from Personal to Collective Healing — How your healing becomes part of something bigger

Each chapter includes reflection prompts, practical tools, language you can use, and stories that will help you see yourself more clearly — and more lovingly.

This book is about remembering, remembering your voice before it was edited, remembering your worth before it was questioned, remembering your dreams before they were downsized, and remembering your dignity is always intact, never needing to be earned.

This book is about healing, not in isolation, but in community. It is about healing, not as a project of perfection, but as a path to liberation; and whether you are a clinician, educator, parent, student, leader, advocate, artist, healer, or simply a human trying to live more freely, this book is for you. This book is about you. And this book is yours.

How to Read This Book

This book is not meant to be read quickly; rather, it is meant to be felt. It is not a textbook, it is a healing companion, and it speaks to your intellect, yes — but also to your heart, your body, your memory, and your imagination.

You can read it cover to cover, or one chapter at a time, or even return to the same page again and again. What matters is not how fast you go — but how deeply you engage.

Here are a few ways to get the most out of it:

1. Bring Your Whole Self

This book invites your thoughts and your emotions, your questions and your lived experiences; and you don't have to agree with everything, but we invite you to stay open, bring your skepticism, bring your longing, and bring your real self.

2. Go Slow

Some sections will stir something inside you; and that's by design. Take your time, pause, reflect, write, walk, and come back when you're ready. For healing is not a race.

3. Use the Prompts

At the end of most chapters, you'll find questions and practices to deepen your experience. These are not homework assignments — they are invitations. Use a journal, speak with a friend, or simply reflect quietly. These practices are where transformation begins.

4. Join or Create a Healing Circle

This book was written in the spirit of community. Healing is amplified in safe, reflective spaces. Consider gathering a small group of peers, family, clients, students, or colleagues, to read and reflect together. Use the circle prompts in the appendix if helpful.

5. Repeat as Needed

Rewriting your inner dialogue is not a one-time process.
This book is designed to be returned to — like a mirror, a map, and a self-affirming statement.

6. Let It Speak to Different Parts of You

You might read this book as a person healing from your own inner critic; or as a clinician helping others recognize theirs; or as a leader trying to create trauma-informed, dignity-based systems; or as someone doing all three. However you enter this book, you are welcome, you belong here, and your journey is precious.

How This Book Works

This book is not just something to read, it's something to experience. Each part, each chapter, and each section is designed to guide you, gently and bravely, through the process of recognizing, disrupting, and rewriting the inner narratives shaped by oppression.
It draws from clinical wisdom, lived experience, liberation psychology, narrative therapy, applied neuroscience, and collective healing practices.

You'll notice a rhythm throughout the book:

1. The Circle Structure

This book is written in the spirit of a healing circle.
Every chapter is like a seat in that circle, a space for honesty, reflection, and transformation.
The circle isn't hierarchical. No chapter is "above" another. You don't have to be an expert to begin. Your presence is enough.

2. The Four-Part Healing Process

At the heart of this book is a clear, repeatable process — The Four Steps of Inner Liberation:

- Awareness – Hearing the inner voice you've been living with
- Disruption – Interrupting that voice with courage and clarity
- Replacement – Planting new inner dialogue rooted in truth and dignity
- Repetition – Practicing new language until it becomes your new way of being

Each chapter contributes to this arc, some chapters focus more on insight, while others offer tools, stories, or language; and they all are part of the process.

3. Personal Reflection and Practice

At the end of most chapters, you'll find:

- Reflection prompts — to help you connect the material to your own life
- Mini-practices — simple, powerful exercises you can do anytime
- Affirming language — to begin replacing harmful inner scripts

You don't have to do every prompt. You don't have to do them in order.
Just engage with what resonates — and come back to what doesn't, when you're ready.

4. Designed for Personal and Collective Use

You can read this book on your own, or in community. It's equally effective in a private journal or a public circle.
It's used by:
- Individuals healing from internalized oppression
- Clinicians supporting clients
- Educators, mentors, and parents modeling new narratives
- Organizers and leaders cultivating collective care

If you're reading as part of a group, check out the Circle Prompts in the appendix.

5. Real Voices, Real Change

Throughout the book, you'll find reflections, insights, and lived experiences from SWEET clinicians, healing circle participants, and the authors themselves. These voices are authentic. They model vulnerability, courage, and the power of rewriting the script — together.

This book doesn't promise to do the work for you; rather, it will walk with you, it will hold up a mirror — not to show you what's wrong, but to remind you of what's always been whole, possible, and yours.

Acknowledgments

This book is the result of many voices, lives, and legacies. It stands on the shoulders of those who dared to tell the truth, even when it cost them everything.

To every individual who has struggled under the weight of internalized oppression and still chose healing: thank you. Your resilience is the foundation of this work.

To our ancestors, known and unknown—those who survived, resisted, dreamed, and loved in the face of unimaginable harm: may your wisdom continue to guide us as we break the chains within.

To the clinicians, educators, activists, and mentors who continue to challenge injustice from the inside out: your courage to model liberation is the medicine our world so deeply needs.

To the SWEET Institute community—for your commitment to healing, equity, and radical empathy. You've made it possible to co-create a new language of care, dignity, and transformation.

To the artists, editors, and designers who helped shape this book's message visually and emotionally: your contributions brought this vision to life in a way that words alone could not.

And to every reader: thank you for choosing to do the inner work. You are not only rewriting your own script—you are shaping a more liberated world for all of us.

With deep respect,
Mardoche Sidor, MD
Adaiah Lasalle, LCSW
Karen Dubin, PhD, LCSW
SWEET Institute

Prologue: The Revolution Starts Within

The room is quiet, save for the steady hum of an old radiator. Chairs are arranged in a circle, worn but welcoming. A candle flickers softly in the center. Six people sit in silence, the kind of silence heavy with unspoken words.

The Elder, Amara, leans forward, elbows resting on their knees, eyes gentle but sharp.

Amara:
"Before we begin, I want to ask you something simple. Not easy — but simple. Whose voice is in your head when you think of yourself? Who do you hear?"

No one speaks at first. They exchange glances, shift in their seats, as if searching for permission.

Ari stares at the floor, chewing on their lip.

Ari:
"I hear… my mother's voice, sometimes. But also… this other voice, bigger than her, like the world itself. Telling me I have to be perfect. Twice as good. Or I'll disappear."

Amara nods slowly.

Amara:
"And does that voice sound like love? Or does it sound like fear?"

Ari hesitates. *"Fear."*

Maria clears her throat, softly.

Maria:
"Mine tells me to stay small. To be grateful for what little I have. That speaking up is dangerous, selfish even. I thought it was just my culture, but… maybe it's more than that."

Sam crosses their arms, defensive.

Sam:
"I don't know. I just know I'm tired. Tired of fighting the same battle every day. Tired of feeling like a stranger in my own skin."

Malik, who has been silent, finally speaks.

Malik:
"The voice told me a long time ago that I was a threat. A danger. That's how they looked at me in the courtroom, at school, even in my own neighborhood. After a while, I stopped questioning it. I started living it."

A long pause.

Grace, softly.

Grace:
"I'm not sure whose voice it is, but it tells me I have to fix everything. That if I get it wrong, I'm just making it worse. And that maybe… maybe I'm part of the problem."

Amara closes their eyes, then opens them again.

Amara:
"These voices you speak of? They're not truly yours. They are the world's echo. Planted by systems older than all of us. Racism. Sexism. Classism. Fear. Control. Colonization. Survival. They have names. They have histories. And they are loud — not just in your mind, but in the minds of many."

The group listens. Some lean forward.

Amara:
"But what if I told you this — the voices can be unlearned. Unwound. Not erased. We do not erase what we've lived. But you do not have to carry them as truth any longer. You are allowed to rewrite the script."

The candle flickers as if to punctuate the words.

Amara:
"This circle is not just about telling stories, or even about understanding. It is about remembering. Remembering who you were before the world told you who to be."

The room feels different now. Warmer. Heavy, still — but with the weight of possibility.

Amara:
"You are not here by accident. Nor are you reading this by accident, friend. Whether you sit here with us in flesh or you hold these pages quietly in your own space, you are part of this circle now. And together, we will begin."

The circle breathes, as one.

The revolution begins.

Dear Reader,
This book is your seat in the circle. As you read, you will hear these voices unfold. Their struggles will feel like yours. Their victories, too. And along the way, you will be invited — gently but firmly — to face your own inner dialogue, to question it, and to rewrite it.
You do not walk alone.

Come, take your place.

Part I: The Origins of the Inner Critic

Chapter 1 — The Oppressor's Voice in Our Heads

The Origins of Internalized Oppression

The circle reconvenes the following week. The same chairs, the same flickering candle, the same quiet hum in the room — but something is different. The silence now feels like anticipation.

Amara begins, as always, with a question.

Amara:
"How does oppression speak when no one is around? What does it say when you are alone, behind closed doors, just you and your thoughts?"

Ari looks up first.

Ari:
"It sounds like me."

The group listens.

Ari:
"It's not someone shouting at me from the outside. It's my own voice saying, you'll never be good enough. No matter what you do. No matter how hard you try. You'll always have to prove yourself — and still, it won't be enough."

A hush falls over the circle. The words land heavily.

Maria:
"It's strange, isn't it? How you start to believe it's your own voice. For me, it says, you don't belong here. Especially when I'm around people with more money, more education. It tells me I'm just a maid, a single mother who should be grateful for anything at all."

She clutches her scarf as if steadying herself.

Sam:
"For me, it whispers you'll always be too much for some people, and not enough for others. It tells me I'll never find a place where I fit — because I wasn't meant to."

Malik clears his throat.

Malik:
"It's like walking with a shadow. Mine says, you're dangerous. Don't forget it. Even when I've done nothing wrong, even when I'm just standing there."

His voice falters. *"I started believing it when I was a kid. And the saddest part? I still do."*

Grace:
"I thought I was supposed to have figured this out. I'm trained to help people through their inner struggles. But when I hear that voice, it says, you don't really belong here either. It tells me I'm either part of the problem, or I don't know enough to help anyone."

Amara watches the circle, eyes soft but focused.

Amara:
"This voice you each describe — the one that calls you unworthy, too much, not enough, dangerous, broken — is not yours."

She lets the words settle.

Amara:
"It's a voice given to you. Sometimes wrapped in a mother's warning, sometimes a teacher's gaze, sometimes the silence after injustice. It is the oppressor's voice — internalized. Spoken now in your own tongue."

Ari:
"So we're... carrying their voice? Thinking it's ours?"

Amara:
"Yes."

The group sits still.

Amara:
"Oppression is not only what happens to you — it is what you begin to believe about yourself because of what happens to you."

Maria:
"But I thought it was me. My thoughts."

Amara:
"That is how internalized oppression works. It's not content just to govern systems. It takes root inside us. It whispers until it sounds like the truth. But you were born without it. None of you arrived in this world with these beliefs. They were taught."

Sam:
"Then why do I still listen?"

Amara:
"Because it's safer — or at least, it feels that way. If you believe you're unworthy, you stop asking for more. If you believe you're a threat, you shrink. If you believe you'll never belong, you stop trying. And the system stays intact."

The candle flickers.

Amara:
"The greatest trick oppression plays is convincing you that its voice is your own."

Malik:
"So what do we do?"

Amara smiles softly.

Amara:
"First, we name it. We name the oppressor's voice. We begin to hear it clearly, as something separate from ourselves."

Reflection for the Reader: Who Do You Hear?
Take a quiet moment.

Whose voice do you hear when you say, I am not enough, I don't belong, I will never succeed, or I'm not allowed to rest?

- Where did you first hear it?
- Who repeated it?
- Who modeled it, lived it, enforced it?

Write it down. No judgment. Only witnessing.

Remember, you were not born speaking this way to yourself. It was given to you.

And what is given can be returned.

The circle sits in silence, but it is no longer the silence of avoidance — it is the silence of recognition.

They are no longer alone with the voice.

They are hearing it together.

And that is where healing begins.

Additional Reflection for the Reader:

Listening for the Voice Inside

Take a quiet moment. Breathe deeply. You are entering precious work.

Ask yourself:
1. What is the voice inside me usually saying when I feel afraid, ashamed, or invisible?
2. When did I first notice this voice? Was I a child? A teenager? An adult?
3. Whose voice does it resemble? Is it mine? Or someone else's?
4. Have I ever questioned it? Or have I lived as if it were true?
5. What has this voice cost me? (Joy, confidence, connection, rest?)
6. What has it protected me from? (Rejection, attention, punishment?)

Now, gently place your hand on your heart and ask:

- What would I say to a dear friend or child who carried this voice?
- Can I allow myself the same kindness?

Finally, take a breath.
Simply noticing is the first step to liberation.

Recognizing the internalized "oppressor" voice that constantly criticizes and undermines us.

Chapter 2 — Systems That Shape Our Souls

Race, Gender, Class, and the Origins of the Inner Critic

The circle gathers again, the candle burning low, casting soft shadows on the walls.

Amara enters without a word and takes their seat. The group follows, settling into the familiar rhythm.

Amara breaks the silence gently.

Amara:
"Last time, we began listening to the voice inside. Today, I want to ask — where did that voice learn to speak? Where did it come from?"

Ari shifts, brows furrowed.

Ari:
"You mean... like, my mom? School?"

Amara:
"And where did your mother learn it? Where did your teachers learn it? Where did this language first enter your family, your community, your skin?"

The circle leans in.

Amara:
"We carry more than just personal wounds. We carry the weight of systems. Some of them have existed for hundreds of years. They shaped your parents, your grandparents, and now, they shape you."

Maria crosses her arms tightly.

Maria:

"In my house, the women always served. Quiet, obedient, tired. They worked, cooked, kept everyone else afloat, and no one said thank you. They didn't even expect it. It's just... what women did. I thought it was just my mother. But now I see — it's older than her."

Sam nods.

Sam:

"Same. I thought my shame came just from my parents, but it's more than that. The world around me — schools, doctors, the church — they all told me who I was allowed to be. And who I wasn't. When everyone you meet speaks the same lie, you start calling it truth."

Malik lowers his eyes.

Malik:

"I grew up hearing stories about how the police did my uncle wrong. About the jobs we couldn't get. About how we had to be careful just walking down the street. And after a while, I stopped dreaming big. Stopped thinking there was a way out. It wasn't one person's fault — it was the air we breathed."

Grace swallows hard.

Grace:

"For me, it's different but the same. I wasn't told I was worthless, but I was told I was better. Better than the kids who lived across the tracks, better than the ones who didn't speak English well, better than girls who were too loud. I never questioned it — it felt normal. But it taught me to disconnect from others... and even from parts of myself."

The circle is still, the truth hanging heavy.

Amara:

"You, see? These voices didn't appear out of thin air. They were built by systems — racism, sexism, classism, homophobia, ableism. Systems that wanted order, control, and silence. Systems that needed you to

*believe you were less than, or that others were. Not for your benefit —
but for theirs."*

Amara pauses, eyes warm but steady.

Amara:
*"This is what we call internalized oppression. It is what happens when
the outside world's judgments are no longer just out there, but in
here."*

Ari:
"So, it's not just me messing up. I inherited this."

Amara:
*"You did. We all did. Not because you were weak. But because you
were human. We are shaped by what surrounds us — and by what
shaped those who came before us."*

Maria whispers.

Maria:
*"So maybe my mother didn't betray me. Maybe she was just trying to
survive."*

Amara:
"Exactly."

Amara leans back, letting the silence settle.

Amara:
*"You are carrying systems inside you. But they are not you. And what
is learned... can be unlearned."*

Reflection for the Reader: Mapping the System

Close your eyes and ask:
- What messages did your parents, teachers, or elders give you about who you are?
- Where did they learn those messages?
- Were they shaped by race, gender, class, or other systems?
- Can you trace the threads?

Write what you find.

See if you can name one message you carry that belongs to a system — not to your truth.

You are allowed to question it.
You are allowed to begin giving it back.

Reflection for the Reader:

Listening for the Voice Inside — Beyond People, Into Systems

Find a quiet space. Breathe deeply. Let yourself notice without judgment.

1. What does the voice inside me often say when I feel afraid, ashamed, or unworthy?
2. When did I first notice this voice? Was it in childhood? In a particular environment? Through repeated experiences?
3. Whose voice does it sound like?
   a. Is it the voice of a parent, teacher, or community member?
   b. Or does it feel like the voice of the culture — a collective expectation?
   c. Could it be the voice of media, religion, or social systems?
   d. Have I absorbed messages about who I am allowed to be from what I saw, not just what I was told?
4. Were there moments when I didn't hear the voice, but felt it?
   a. In the absence of representation?
   b. In stereotypes I witnessed but didn't question?
   c. In rules that were unspoken but clearly enforced?

5. How has this voice shaped what I believe about:
    a. My worth
    b. My safety
    c. My belonging
    d. My potential
6. What has this voice protected me from?
    a. Have I obeyed it to avoid rejection, punishment, invisibility, or danger?
7. What has this voice cost me?
    a. Joy?
    b. Rest?
    c. Full self-expression?
    d. Dreams?
8. If I could speak directly to this voice today, what would I want to say?
9. If I could rewrite the script today, what would I most need to hear?

Reflection for the Reader (Liberation-Informed Version)

Listening for the Voice Inside — Naming the Systemic Sources

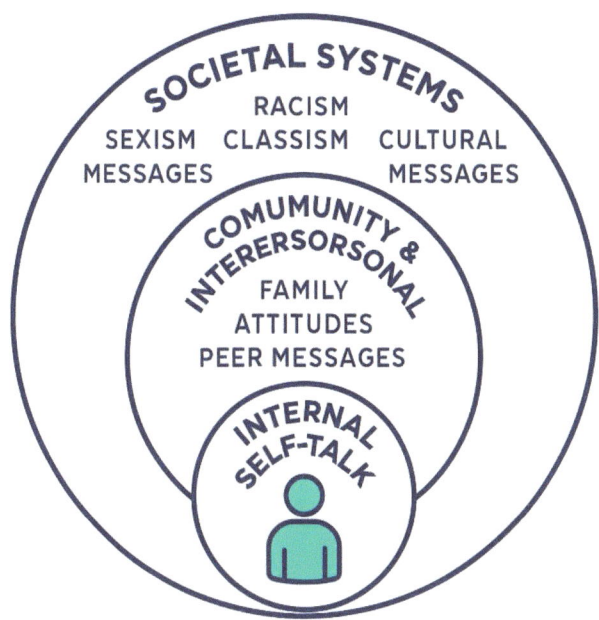

Take a few quiet breaths. Settle into stillness.

1. What does the voice inside me usually say when I am afraid, ashamed, or unsure of myself?
2. When did this voice first begin to speak? Was I young? Was it tied to a particular event, relationship, or environment?
    a. Whose voice does it resemble?
    b. Is it the voice of a parent, caregiver, teacher, or community member?
    c. Or does it echo the voice of the larger world — through media, religious teachings, school systems, or laws?
    d. Could it come from unspoken rules about how I should behave, look, or succeed?
3. How have systems shaped this voice?
    a. Did race play a role?

     b. Did gender, sexual orientation, or gender identity play a role?

     c. Did class, immigration status, or ability shape how I saw myself?

4. What messages did I absorb — directly or indirectly — about people like me?

5. How have these messages influenced:
   a. What I believe I am allowed to do or become?
   b. How much space I believe I can take up?
   c. What I believe I must sacrifice or perform to be accepted or safe?

6. How did these messages feel in my body?
   a. Did I shrink?
   b. Did I become vigilant?
   c. Did I try to disappear or overcompensate?
   d. Did I begin to police myself before anyone else could?

7. What has this voice protected me from?
   a. Have I used it as a survival strategy to stay safe, loved, or invisible?

8. What has it cost me?
   a. Joy?
   b. Freedom?
   c. Full self-expression?
   d. Rest?

9. If I could speak kindly to this voice — knowing it tried to protect me — what would I want to say now?

10. What do I want to believe about myself moving forward?

As the candle dims, the circle sits quietly. No one rushes to speak. They are tracing threads that were always there but never named.

The revolution has already begun.

Chapter 3 — From Microaggressions to Mental Imprisonment

How Chronic Invalidation Shapes Our Inner Dialogue

The circle returns on a rainy evening. The room smells faintly of wet earth and chamomile tea. Everyone seems quieter than usual, like they have been carrying new questions since the last gathering.

Amara waits until each person is settled before speaking.

Amara:
"What happens when you hear the same message, not once, but again and again? What happens when it shows up every day — not as a scream, but as a whisper? As a look? A pause? An omission?"

Sam is the first to speak.

Sam:
"It wears you down. That's what happens. It's not always outright violence. It's the small things. The cashier calling me sir even after I correct them. The teacher ignoring my hand. The silence when I try to talk about who I am."

Sam glances down, eyes watery.

Sam:
"It's like being erased, one little stroke at a time."

Maria nods, her voice low.

Maria:
"I feel that too. When I speak up in meetings and people act like I'm invisible. When I'm praised only when I'm quiet. Or when I'm told, you're not like the others, like it's a compliment. It's... humiliating."

Ari:
"And sometimes it's not even words. It's the security guard following me around the store. The white lady clutching her purse on the train. The boss saying we're looking for someone more professional, and you just know what they mean."

A pause. Malik, who has been quiet, looks up.

Malik:
"Or the look they give your son when he's only ten but already treated like he's guilty of something. That look. That look says more than words ever could."

The circle breathes together.

Grace:
"I see it too. Sometimes I'm the one giving it. Not on purpose — but when I'm honest, I notice how I act differently depending on who's in the room. Even when I don't want to. It's like the system lives in me, too."

Amara leans forward.

Amara:
"These are what we call microaggressions. Small, subtle — but never harmless. They are the thousand tiny cuts of oppression. Over time, they don't just shape how the world sees you. They shape how you see yourself."

Sam:
"Yeah. After a while, you start seeing yourself through their eyes. You catch yourself avoiding the places where you know you'll get those looks. You stop speaking up. You shrink."

Maria:
"You blame yourself. You think, maybe I was too loud, maybe I took up too much space, maybe I should have known better."

Amara:
"And you start carrying the burden for the very systems that wounded you."

The room is heavy now. The group realizes it's not just about grand moments of injustice — it's about the slow, daily wearing down of the soul.

Ari:
"I thought I was just tired because of work. But maybe I'm tired from carrying this every day. Without even realizing it."

Malik:
"Same. I've been blaming myself for being so guarded, so careful. But how can you not be when every room feels like it's watching you?"

Amara:
"This is how the inner critic grows. Not from one moment, but from thousands. When the outside whispers enough times, you begin to whisper it to yourself."

Amara lets the silence hold them.

Amara:
"But you must know this:
You were not meant to live small.
You were not born to believe you are less.
The voices you hear inside were planted — and what is planted, if unwanted, can be uprooted."

The group exhales, slowly.

Amara:
"Our work is not just to survive the outer world, but to reclaim the inner one."

Reflection for the Reader: Counting the Unseen
Take a few quiet breaths.

Think about the micro-messages you've received.
- When did someone ignore you, doubt you, dismiss you, or make you feel less than?
- How often did it happen?
- What story did those moments start telling inside you?

Write them down — not to relive the pain, but to see it clearly.

This is not your fault.
This is what the world has whispered — but you don't have to repeat it.

Reflection for the Reader: Tracking the Impact of Microaggressions
Take a moment to breathe. You are invited to become a witness to your own experience — with gentleness and clarity.
1. Think of a recent moment when you experienced a microaggression.
   a. What happened?
   b. What wasn't said, but was clearly communicated?
   c. What did your internal dialogue sound like in that moment?
   d. Did you question yourself?
   e. Did you feel pressure to stay quiet, minimize it, or explain it away?
2. How did you respond inside your body?
   a. Tightening?
   b. Numbness?
   c. Shame?
   d. Rage without a place to go?
3. What story did that moment reinforce about you?
   a. That you're too sensitive?
   b. That you don't belong?
   c. That you have to work twice as hard to be seen or safe?
   d. Now look at the cumulative pattern:

4. What messages have you internalized after experiencing microaggressions again and again?
   a. Do these messages sound like your voice — or were they planted there?
5. How do systems reinforce this voice?
6. What does whiteness, patriarchy, capitalism, ableism, or cisnormativity demand of you in order to be deemed acceptable?
7. Have you ever noticed yourself anticipating microaggressions before they happen — and adjusting your behavior or self-talk in advance?
8. What has that done to your trust in your own perception, your voice, or your right to take up space?
9. If your inner voice has echoed the harm of microaggressions, what might it sound like to speak back with truth and dignity?
10. What would it feel like to trust your experience — fully?

The circle sits together, eyes glassy, but backs a little straighter. Naming what was unseen changes everything.

They are beginning to hear themselves — beyond the noise.

The healing deepens.

FROM MICROAGGRESSIONS TO

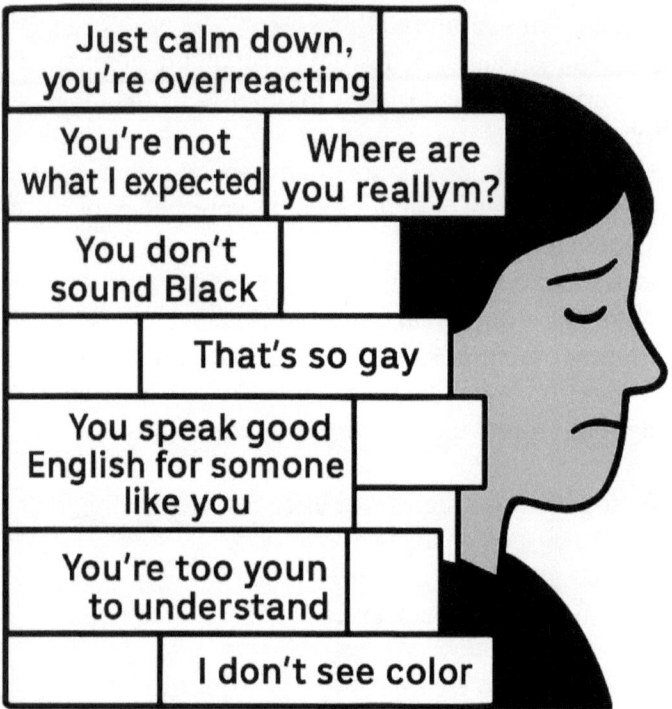

MENTAL IMPRISONMENT

Chapter 4 — Naming the Inner Narratives

Recognizing the Scripts We've Been Living

The circle meets again under a warmer sky. The window is cracked open, and the air carries the smell of new blossoms. There is a sense of quiet strength in the room — like something is beginning to shift beneath the surface.

Amara enters and lights the candle in the center. This time, instead of opening with a question, they hold up a small, folded piece of paper.

Amara:
"Inside this paper are three sentences. I want you to hear them. Not just with your ears, but with your body. Tell me if you recognize them."

They unfold the paper, then read slowly, one by one:

Amara:
"I'll never be enough."
"I can't afford to rest."
"It's my fault."

A murmur moves through the circle like a wave.
Maria exhales sharply.

Maria:
"I've said all three. So many times I didn't even realize I was saying them."

Sam:
"That second one? I can't afford to rest. That's me. I hear it every time I start to slow down, even when my body is screaming for a break. It's like resting is... dangerous."

Grace:
"For me, it's the third one. It's my fault. Even when I try to help and things don't work out, I internalize it. I carry guilt for things I didn't create."

Ari leans forward.

Ari:
"I hear I'll never be enough like a loop. At work. At home. Even when I accomplish something, the voice just says, not quite. And then I hustle harder, hoping to shut it up."

Malik speaks slowly.

Malik:
"My script used to be you're dangerous. But now it's changed. Now it says, don't expect too much. Like, if I keep my hopes low, I won't get hurt."

Amara nods, gently.

Amara:
"These are what we call inner narratives. They are like scripts, written by experience, repetition, and survival. Often invisible. Often unquestioned. And they shape everything — how you speak, love, work, rest, and even dream."

Maria:
"So, we're living out a story we didn't even write?"

Amara:
"Yes. But here's the truth: once you see the script, you no longer have to follow it."

They pause.

Amara:
"But first, you must name it."

The circle is quiet. The moment feels sacred — like something old is being touched for the first time.

Amara:
"Each of you has a dominant inner narrative. One that guides your choices, shapes your fears, defines your limits. You've lived by it for so long it may feel like your identity. But it is not. It is a survival response. Not your essence."

Sam:
"How do we find it?"

Amara:
"Listen to what you say to yourself when you are afraid. When you make a mistake. When you feel ashamed. The script will appear there. Quiet, but consistent."

Grace:
"What do we do once we name it?"

Amara:
"We challenge it. But not by force. By truth. You don't need to argue with the narrative — you need to show it who you really are. That takes time. And practice. And love."

Ari:
"So, naming it is the first act of liberation?"

Amara:
"Exactly."

Reflection for the Reader: What's Your Script?

Take a few breaths. Settle into stillness. Ask yourself:
- What sentence plays in your mind when you make a mistake?
- What belief holds you back when an opportunity arises?
- What do you whisper to yourself when no one is watching?

Here are a few examples:
- I'm too much.
- I don't deserve to be here.
- If I speak up, I'll be punished.
- I should know better by now.
- People like me don't get that kind of life.
- I must be useful to be loved.

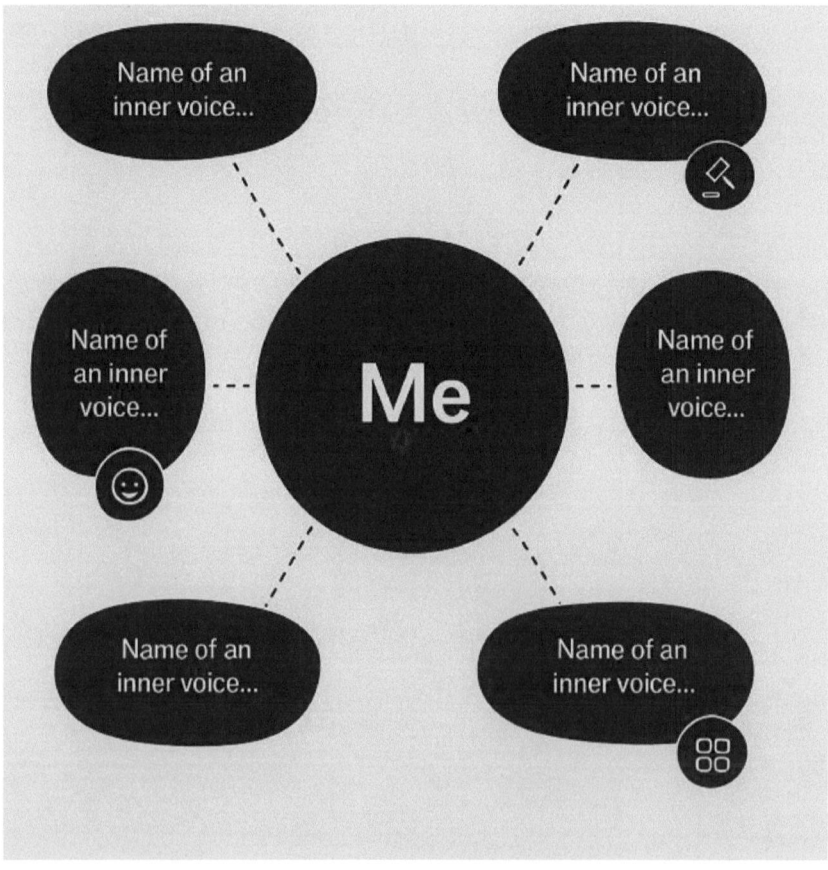

Write yours down. Speak it aloud.
Then ask:

- Where did I first hear this?
- Whose voice taught me this?
- Does it belong to me — or to the world that shaped me?

Naming it does not mean you believe it.
It means you are ready to set it down.

The circle sits still, some writing, some weeping, some simply breathing.
They are no longer living unnamed stories.
They are authors now — not of the past, but of what comes next.

Reflection for the Reader: Naming — and Now What?

You've begun to hear the voice more clearly. Now, let's sit with it a little longer — not to dwell, but to learn, to reclaim, and to begin choosing differently.

1. What inner narratives have been most persistent in your life?
   a. (I'm not enough, I have to earn love, I don't belong, If I rest, I fail)
2. Where do you believe these came from?
   a. A parent or caregiver?
   b. A community norm?
   c. School?
   d. Religious teachings?
   e. Media?
   f. Laws or cultural silences?
3. How have these narratives influenced the way you:
   a. Speak to yourself?
   b. Enter relationships?
   c. Make decisions?
   d. Take up space — or don't?
4. How do these scripts benefit you today?
   a. Do they keep you safe, hidden, or in control?

5. How do these scripts limit you today?
6. What have they cost you in terms of freedom, joy, or authenticity?

Now, Gently Ask: What Can I Do with These Narratives?

1. Can I question them — not to fight them, but to explore them?
2. Can I externalize them — write them down, speak them aloud, or imagine setting them outside of me?
3. Can I thank them — for how they tried to protect me — and still decide I don't need to keep obeying them?
4. Can I replace them — even with small words that feel more true?
5. What would my inner voice sound like if it were rooted in compassion, truth, and dignity — instead of fear?

Chapter 5 — The Mirror is Distorted

How Internalized Oppression Warps Self-Image and Relationships

The circle gathers under the soft glow of early evening. There is a different energy tonight — heavier but determined. They've named the inner voices. Now comes the harder question: What has believing them done?

Amara's eyes move slowly around the circle before speaking.

Amara:
"When you look in the mirror — I do not mean the glass one — but the mirror of your own mind... who do you see? And is it really you?"

The group fidgets, exchanging glances. No one wants to go first.

Ari finally breaks the silence.

Ari:
"I see someone who is not enough. Not enough to lead. Not enough to rest. Not enough to mess up without being punished." Their voice tightens. *"Even when people compliment me, I don't trust it. I assume they don't mean it, or they don't see the real me — the flawed one."*

Maria:
"Same. I see someone who needs to prove herself. I overwork, over-give, even when no one is asking. And when I don't? I feel like I'm failing. Like I'm selfish."

She wipes her eyes quickly.

Sam:
"I don't even recognize the person in the mirror most days. Some days, I see someone who is wrong. Not just different — wrong. Like the body isn't mine. Like I'm disappointing everyone by existing."

The circle holds its breath.

Malik:
"I see a threat. That's what the world told me. And now I expect people to fear me. I walk into rooms already assuming I'm dangerous. I hear myself say, Don't speak too loud. Don't stand too tall."

Grace:
"For me, it's not just about being enough. It's about always needing to fix, to apologize, to take responsibility for everyone's pain — even when it's not mine to carry."

Amara leans back, letting their words ripple across the circle.

Amara:
"These are the distortions. This is how oppression bends the mirror. You are not seeing yourself — you are seeing yourself through the lens of a system designed to shrink you, control you, or burden you with guilt."

Sam:
"So, we've been taught to see a false version of ourselves?"

Amara:
"Yes. And the tragedy is, you've been relating to this false image as if it were the truth. You've made decisions based on it. Built relationships around it. Shrunk or contorted yourself to fit it."

Maria:
"No wonder I'm so tired."

Amara:
"Tiredness is not just from doing too much — it is from being too small for too long. You were never meant to live inside a distorted mirror."

The group sits in quiet shock.

Amara:

"But hear this — and hear it fully: you are not broken. You have adapted. You have survived. The image you carry is a strategy, not a flaw."

Ari:

"So, what do we do? We can't just throw the mirror away."

Amara:

"No, you don't throw it away. You clean it. You see what's behind it. Slowly, gently, you remove the layers that do not belong to you. The dust is not you. The distortion is not you."

Malik:

"But it feels so real."

Amara:

"It will. At first. But just because you've lived with it doesn't mean you must continue to live by it. Distortion, no matter how familiar, is not destiny."

Reflection for the Reader: The Mirror Exercise

The Mirror is Distorted

Distorted Mirror (Internalized View)	Clear Mirror (Authentic View)
I only got here by mistake; I don't belong	I have earned my place and I belong here
I'm just being too sensitive	My feelings are valid
My natural hair is unprofessional	My appearance is professional and reflects who I am
I'm not smart enough	I am intelligent and capable

Take a moment. Close your eyes.
Ask yourself:
- How do you see yourself — truly?
- Is the image kind, honest, and whole? Or is it harsh, small, fearful?
- What if this image isn't the real you, but a reflection shaped by years of distorted messages?

Write down:
- What you tend to believe about yourself.
- What you suspect may be the distortion, not the truth.
- What you long to see when you look inward.

Remember, you are not the distortion.
You are what's underneath it.

Additional Reflection for the Reader: Seeing Through the Distortion

You have begun to name the voice — now it's time to notice how that voice has shaped the way you see yourself.

1. When you picture yourself — emotionally, physically, spiritually — what do you see?
    a. Is the image kind, honest, and whole?
    b. Or is it shaped by fear, judgment, or shame?
2. What beliefs do you hold about who you are — and where did those beliefs come from?
    a. I'm too much
    b. I'll always be behind
    c. I'm the fixer, the strong one
    d. No one really sees me
    e. I have to be perfect to be safe
3. What external sources contributed to these beliefs?
    a. Racialized expectations?
    b. Gender roles or body stereotypes?
    c. Messages about class, ability, sexuality, or language?
    d. Media portrayals that erased or misrepresented people like you?
4. Have you ever felt pressure to perform a version of yourself in order to belong, succeed, or be safe?
5. What emotions come up when you consider that your mirror may have been distorted — not by your flaws, but by someone else's lens?

Now Ask: How Can I Begin to See Myself More Clearly?
1. What moments — however rare — have felt like a glimpse of your truest self?
    a. A moment of joy?
    b. Stillness?
    c. Creative flow?
    d. Connection?
2. What would it feel like to see yourself through the eyes of someone who loves you without condition?
3. If your distorted self-image was based on fear, what would a more loving image look like — even if you're not ready to fully believe it yet?
4. Can you name three truths about yourself that are not based on performance, productivity, or pleasing others?
5. What practices (mirror work, affirmations, movement, storytelling, ancestral remembering) might help you begin to see your full self — not the edited version?

You are not broken.
You are learning to see.
The distortion is not your identity — it is the residue of a system.
And you are already beginning to wipe the mirror clean.

The circle breathes deeply. The silence is no longer filled with shame, but with the quiet realization that maybe, just maybe, who they thought they were is not who they really are.

The healing has begun to touch the root.

Part II
The Psychology of Liberation: How Internalized Oppression Warps Self-Image and Relationships

Chapter 6 — When Silence Becomes a Survival Strategy

Code-Switching, Shrinking, and the Cost of Invisibility

The circle is unusually still today. Everyone seems to feel the same heaviness, but no one is quite ready to name it.

Amara sits quietly, letting the silence stretch, not rushing to fill it.

Amara:
"Let's begin with this: What have you had to hide, shrink, or silence in order to stay safe? To be accepted? To survive?"

The question hangs like smoke.

Grace is the first to speak, her voice measured.

Grace:
"I used to think silence was strength. Like, if I didn't complain, didn't cry, didn't ask for help, then I was in control. I realize now... it was fear. Fear of being seen as weak. Or worse — being told I was taking up too much space."

Maria adds, almost whispering.

Maria:
"I stay quiet a lot. At work, at school meetings, even at church. I don't want to be seen as too loud, too emotional, too Latina. I laugh when things aren't funny. I nod when I disagree. I shrink without even thinking about it."

She pauses, then adds, *"I disappear to stay safe."*

Ari clenches their fists, then releases them.

Ari:
"I've been code-switching since I was ten. Change the way I speak, soften my tone, keep it professional — always professional. I've trained myself to be non-threatening. But it's exhausting. Sometimes I don't even know what my real voice sounds like anymore."

Sam:
"I've spent years trying to make other people comfortable with me. Smiling when I want to scream. Educating people when I'm bleeding. Wearing what feels safe, saying what feels safe. Some days, survival means being silent. But that silence is suffocating."

Malik looks at the ground, jaw tight.

Malik:
"I learned to speak only when asked. I was taught that silence keeps you alive. But now, I can't find my voice even when I want to use it. It's like I handed it over a long time ago."

The room is thick with emotion — not panic, but recognition.

Amara:
"Silence is one of the oldest survival strategies in the book. Oppression doesn't just threaten your body. It trains you to hide your truth. It teaches you that visibility equals danger. So, you learn to stay small, quiet, agreeable. Until you forget what it feels like to take up space."

Grace:
"So, silence isn't weakness. It's protection."

Amara:
"Exactly. But what protects you in one moment can imprison you in the next."

Maria:
"That's what it feels like. A prison I built myself — with good intentions."

Amara:
"That's what all survival strategies are. They are gifts you gave yourself in order to stay alive, stay loved, or stay safe. But eventually, you outgrow them. And they begin to cost you more than they give."

Ari:
"So, what do we do with that? We can't just start shouting from the rooftops. That's not safe either."

Amara:
"True liberation is not about being loud. It's about being authentic. It's about giving yourself permission to exist — fully. And that begins with noticing where you've disappeared — and gently coming back."

Sam:
"Even if it feels dangerous?"

Amara:
"Especially then. But you don't have to do it all at once. Liberation doesn't have to be loud. Sometimes, it starts with a whisper. Sometimes, it starts with saying, I matter, and meaning it — even if only in your own mind."

The group breathes together — a circle of survivors, slowly becoming whole.

**Reflection for the Reader: Where Have You Gone Silent?
Uncovering Strategies of Survival — and Imagining the Shape of
Liberation**

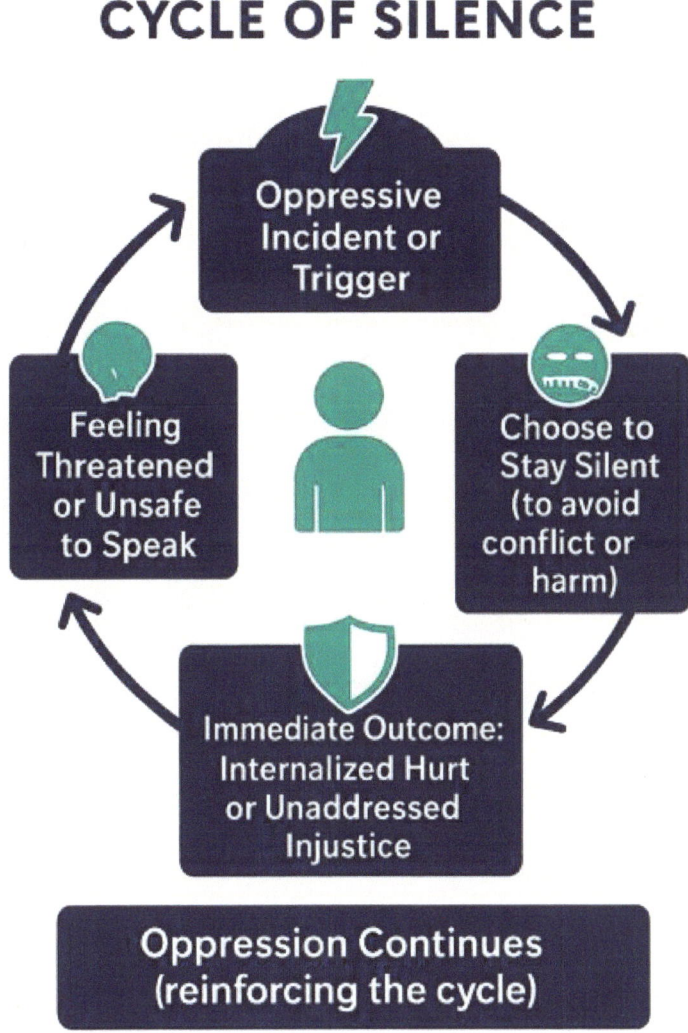

Take a breath. You are not being judged. You are being invited to see yourself clearly — and gently.

1. What parts of yourself have you hidden in order to be accepted, loved, or included?
   a. Your voice?
   b. Your softness?
   c. Your anger?
   d. Your accent?
   e. Your neurodivergence?
   f. Your gender expression?
   g. Your grief or spiritual beliefs?
2. Where do you tend to silence your truth — or shrink your presence?
   a. In relationships?
   b. At work?
   c. In front of authority?
   d. In spiritual or academic spaces?
   e. Even when you're alone?
3. What have you taught yourself to do in order to "stay safe," stay in good favor, or stay unseen? Let the answers come. They might include:
   a. People-pleasing
   b. Over-apologizing
   c. Never resting
   d. Laughing when things aren't funny
   e. Smiling through discomfort
   f. Over-explaining or preemptively justifying yourself
   g. Hiding your needs or minimizing your success
   h. Avoiding eye contact, or making extra effort to appear "non-threatening"
   i. Numbing out — emotionally, intellectually, spiritually
   j. Telling yourself: It's not that bad. I should be grateful. Others have it worse.
4. Who taught you that these strategies were necessary?
   a. Was it a person?
   b. A system?
   c. A repeated lived experience?

Now: Envisioning Freedom
1. Imagine for a moment that the silence is no longer needed.
   a. What does freedom look like in your body?
   b. What does it sound like in your inner voice?
   c. How would you move through the world?
2. What would it feel like to:
   a. Speak without apology?
   b. Set boundaries without guilt?
   c. Rest without justification?
   d. Be seen in your fullness — and not flinch?
3. What relationships would change if you were no longer shrinking?
4. What kind of community would support that kind of freedom — not just tolerate it, but celebrate it?
5. What is one small act you could take this week that moves you closer to that version of yourself?
6. What is one sentence you could say — out loud or in writing — that your silenced self has been longing to hear?

Your silence kept you safe.
But it is not your home.
Freedom is not a performance.
It is the quiet knowing: I am allowed to be here. Fully.

You are remembering.
Now ask:
- Is it still serving me?
- Or is it time to reclaim the space I've surrendered?

Remember:

You did what you had to do to survive.
But survival is not the ceiling.
You are allowed to take up space.

The group sits in a heavy pause. It's not the kind of silence born of fear, but the kind that arrives when something unspoken has finally begun to stir.

Amara looks around the room.
Amara:
"What other voices have taught you to be silent — not just in childhood, but in places you're still moving through now?"

Ari glances down.

Ari:
"At work, when I speak with conviction, I get labeled as 'too intense.' If I share an idea too quickly, I'm 'aggressive.' So, I've trained myself to shrink it down — soften, smile, over-qualify. And after a while, I stop wanting to speak at all."

Maria:
"Same. But for me it's class. I work in spaces where most people talk like they went to Ivy League schools. So I monitor my grammar, I over-explain, I hold my body smaller. There's this voice that says: They're already looking for a reason to think you don't belong."

Sam adds quietly.

Sam:
"Ableism shows up for me in ways people don't even notice. The way meetings are scheduled with no breaks. The way speed is praised. The way needing support is seen as weakness. And over time, the message becomes: Don't speak up about your needs. Don't be a burden."

Malik:
"For me it's my body. The way I look. The assumptions people make. The ways they respond — or don't — before I even open my mouth. And after a while, the silence isn't just something I choose. It becomes the only thing that feels safe."

Grace:

"There's something about being told to be grateful for being included — even when I'm being tokenized. It's like: Be grateful you're at the table. Don't ask for too much. And even if no one says that out loud, I hear it. And I hear it… inside."

The group falls into a stillness again — but this time, a shared one. Their silences were not the same, but they echoed.

Amara:

"These voices are not accidental. They are systemic. They are patterned. They are passed down, and passed around, until we internalize them — not just as beliefs, but as strategies for survival."

Ari:

"And the strategy becomes a habit. And the habit becomes your voice."

Amara:

"Yes. And that is why you're here. To remember — with each other — that silence was a brilliant adaptation. But it is not the truth of who you are."

Additional Reflection for the Reader: Exploring the Silence Within

Take a deep breath. This is not about blame. It's about understanding.
Your silence has a story. Let's listen to it with compassion.

1. When in your life did you first learn that it was safer to stay quiet, agreeable, invisible, or small?
2. What messages did you receive — directly or indirectly — about speaking up, taking up space, or being your full self?
   a. Don't make waves.
   b. Be polite.
   c. People like you are too emotional, too loud, too intense.
   d. Stay in your place.
   e. Be strong. Don't complain.

    f. Be grateful — it could be worse.

    g.

3. From whom did those messages come?
    a. A family member?
    b. A teacher?
    c. A spiritual leader?
    d. A cultural norm?
    e. A system (e.g., school, law, workplace, immigration)?
    f. Social messages tied to your race, gender, class, sexuality, body, or ability?
4. How has silence protected you?
    a. From conflict?
    b. From judgment?
    c. From punishment or exclusion?
5. How has it harmed you?
    a. Have you lost your voice, your clarity, your right to be seen?
    b. Have you ever left situations wishing you had spoken up?

Now Ask: What Could Reclaiming My Voice Look Like?

1. In what spaces do you still silence yourself — even when you have something to say?
2. How would it feel to speak — even in a whisper — your truth?
3. What fears arise?
4. What would safety look like for your voice?
5. Can you recall a moment when you did speak up? What helped you? What happened?
6. What part of you still believes silence is safer — and what part of you is ready for something more whole?
7. What is one small, concrete way you could begin to reclaim your voice this week?
    a. Writing your truth
    b. Naming a boundary
    c. Not apologizing for existing
    d. Saying no or yes without explanation
    e. Speaking kindly to yourself — out loud

Silence has been your strategy.
Now it can become your teacher.
You are not wrong for shrinking.
But you no longer have to.

Your voice is not a threat.
It is a return.

The circle closes in quiet understanding. They are beginning to see
that silence, shrinking, and invisibility were never weaknesses — they
were strategies. But now, the time has come to build something new.

Something real.
Something free.

Chapter 7 — Healing is Resistance

Why Reclaiming Your Mind is an Act of Defiance

The circle feels different tonight. Less guarded. The air is thick with something more tender than the weeks before. A quiet understanding has begun to take root.

Amara sits quietly until the room settles.

Amara:
"What if I told you that healing is not a luxury? It is not selfish. It is not optional. Healing is — and has always been — an act of resistance."

The group looks puzzled.

Ari:
"But isn't healing personal? Like, about me? My mind? My stuff? How is that resistance?"

Amara smiles softly.

Amara:
"Oppression is not just about laws and chains. It is about convincing you that you are less than. That you are broken. That you must stay small. Healing interrupts that narrative. Every time you reclaim your dignity, every time you take up space, every time you believe in your own worth — you are resisting."

Maria leans forward.

Maria:
"I always thought of resistance as marches, protests, speeches. Not... rest. Not saying no when I'm too tired. Not saying I matter."

Amara:
"That is where we have been tricked. The system wants you to believe that the only forms of resistance are the ones that are visible. But the most powerful resistance? Is internal. It is reclaiming what oppression tried to steal: your voice, your joy, your breath."

Sam:
"So, choosing to live as I am, even if it's hard, is resistance?"

Amara:
"Exactly. Being whole in a world that told you to fragment yourself is an act of revolution."

Malik:
"And what about hope? I gave up hope a long time ago. Does hoping count as resistance?"

Amara's eyes soften.

Amara:
"Hope is one of the most radical acts you can perform. Especially for those of us who were told, generation after generation, don't expect too much. To hope is to refuse to accept the limits the world placed on you."

Grace:
"I never saw it like that. I thought the best I could do was help others resist. But I've been neglecting the work inside myself."

Amara:
"Helping others is powerful. But when you abandon yourself in the process, you are not resisting, you are reenacting. Healing is not just for your clients, your family, your community — it is also for you."

A silence spreads, this time tender and soft.

Amara:
"Healing is not selfish. It is the soil where justice grows."

Maria:
"But where do we start?"

Amara:
"You already have.
You showed up.
You spoke.
You listened.
You named.
You felt.
And now, you are remembering.
And every act of remembering who you truly are is resistance."

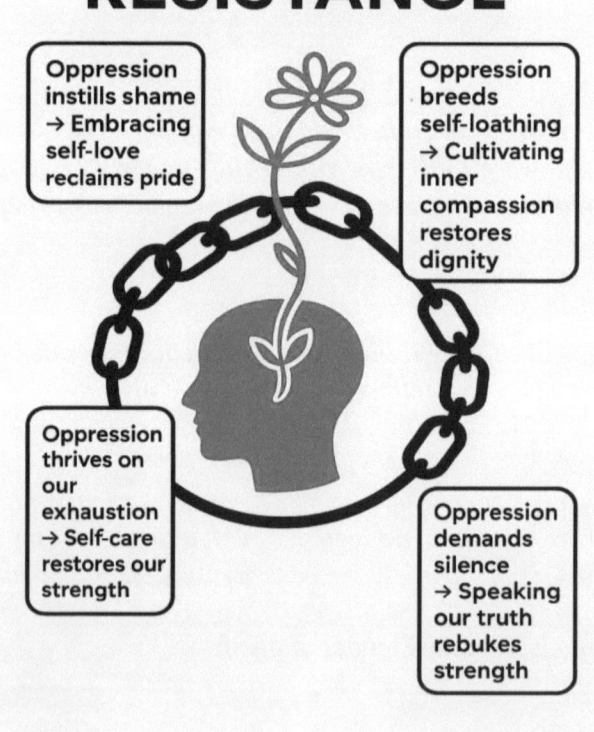

HEALING IS RESISTANCE

Oppression instills shame → Embracing self-love reclaims pride

Oppression breeds self-loathing → Cultivating inner compassion restores dignity

Oppression thrives on our exhaustion → Self-care restores our strength

Oppression demands silence → Speaking our truth rebukes strength

Reflection for the Reader: How is Your Healing Resistance?

Take a quiet moment.
1. In what ways have you believed that healing is selfish, indulgent, or a luxury?
2. Who benefits from you staying tired, silent, ashamed, or afraid?
3. What does your resistance look like today?
   a. Saying no?
   b. Resting without guilt?
   c. Speaking up?
   d. Asking for help?
   e. Feeling joy in a world that tells you not to?

Write it down.

Your healing is not a side project.
It is part of the revolution.
It is the revolution.

Additional Reflection for the Reader: What If Your Healing Is the Revolution?

Reframing Rest, Joy, Boundaries, and Self-Worth as Acts of Defiance

Take a deep breath. Feel into the truth that healing is not a side note.
It is the work.
It is the resistance.

1. What forms of healing have you been taught to feel guilty about or unworthy of?
   a. Rest?
   b. Saying no?
   c. Crying?
   d. Releasing toxic relationships?
   e. Asking for help?
   f. Slowing down?
   g. Choosing joy?
2. What voices have made you feel like healing is indulgent, selfish, or a distraction from your responsibilities?

3. How have systems — like capitalism, racism, patriarchy, colonialism — reinforced the idea that your worth is tied to your pain, your labor, or your silence?
4. Have you ever seen others praised for "pushing through" while your needs were dismissed?
5. What messages have you internalized about survival versus thriving?
    a. Are you allowed to rest before you've earned it?
    b. Do you believe healing has to be painful to be valid?
    c. Do you subconsciously wait for permission to take care of yourself?

Now Ask: What Does Resistance Look Like in My Healing?
1. What is one way I've already practiced resistance by healing — even if I didn't name it that way?
2. What would it look like to trust that my healing is not a delay, but a doorway?
3. What would it mean to speak to myself with tenderness — not as a luxury, but as a radical act?
4. If my ancestors or inner child could speak, would they want me to carry pain — or release it?
5. What is one act of healing I can practice this week that might feel political, spiritual, or personal — or all three?
    Examples:
    - Going to therapy
    - Saying I deserve to be well
    - Taking a nap without guilt
    - Dancing without purpose
    - Eating with reverence
    - Speaking your truth, even if it trembles

You are not selfish for wanting to heal.
You are remembering the part of you that was never broken.

Let that remembering grow.
The circle breathes, and for the first time, someone smiles.
The resistance has already begun.

Chapter 8 — A Language of Liberation

Rewriting the Way We Speak to Ourselves

The circle feels different tonight — softer, but charged. As if everyone knows something is about to change.

Amara enters, places the candle in the center, and says nothing. Instead, they pick up a piece of paper and write on it in silence.

Then, Amara holds it up.
It reads:
I am not enough.

Amara:
"How many of you have said this to yourself?"

All five hands go up.

Amara:
"Tonight, we are going to learn a new language — the language of liberation. But first, we must see how fluent we are in the language of oppression."

The circle leans in.

Amara:
"Tell me the sentences you've said to yourself — quietly, automatically, every day."

Ari speaks without hesitation.

Ari:
"If I mess up, they'll see I don't belong."

Maria:
"Rest is for people who deserve it. I haven't earned it yet."

Sam:
"I'll never be accepted. I'll always be too much."

Malik:
"Don't dream too big. You'll only be disappointed."

Grace:
"I should have done more. I should have known better."

Amara writes them all down on slips of paper and places them gently in the center.

Amara:
"These are not your words. These are the voices you inherited — from systems, families, fear. But here's the good news: Every sentence has an alternative. Every oppressive script has a liberating one."

Amara picks up Ari's sentence.

Amara:
"If I mess up, they'll see I don't belong."

Amara:
"What if the truth is: I am allowed to make mistakes and still belong."

Ari's eyes well up.

Amara picks up Maria's.

Amara:
"Rest is for people who deserve it."

Amara:
"What if the truth is: Rest is my birthright, not a reward."

Maria gasps softly.

Amara continues.

Amara:
"I'll never be accepted." (Sam's) "What if: I am worthy of love as I am."

Sam:
"But what if the world disagrees?"

Amara:
"Let the world catch up. Your liberation cannot wait for their approval."

Malik wipes his eyes.

Malik:
"So, I can say, I am allowed to dream. Even if it feels foolish?"

Amara:
"Yes, Malik. And every time you say it, you are reclaiming stolen ground."

Grace:
"I should have done more."

Amara gently counters.

Amara:
"What if: I did what I could, and I am allowed to grow."

Grace covers her face, tears quietly falling.

Amara:
"Liberation is not only something you march for. It is something you speak. It is how you talk to yourself — when no one is listening."

Ari:
"But won't it feel like lying? I've said the other things for so long."

Amara:
"It will feel unfamiliar — not because it's untrue, but because you have not been taught your own language yet."

Sam:
"So, we're learning to speak again."

Amara:
"Yes. And every sentence you rewrite is a door you unlock."

Reflection for the Reader: Rewrite One Sentence
Choose one sentence you often tell yourself.

Write it here:
I tell myself…

Now, gently — without forcing — offer an alternative:
The liberating truth might be…

Repeat this sentence aloud.

It does not have to feel natural yet.
It only has to be yours, not inherited.
This is how you begin to learn the language of liberation.

FROM OPPRESSIVE SELF-TALK TO LANGUAGE OF LIBERATION

FROM OPPRESSIVE SEL-TALK	TO LANGUAGE OF LIBERATION
I should just stay invisible	My voice and presence matter.
I can't do anything right	I can learn and grow
I'm being too sensitive, it's not a big deal	My feelings are valid and signal real issues
I'm a failure	I am resilient

Additional Reflection for the Reader: Practicing a New Voice

Rewriting Inner Dialogue with Truth, Compassion, and Power

You've begun to notice the voice.
You've named it.
Now, you are being invited to speak back — not to silence it, but to liberate yourself from it.

1. What sentence do you most often say to yourself that you now realize is rooted in internalized oppression?

Examples:
- a. I'm not enough
- b. I'll never be accepted
- c. If I rest, I'll fall behind
- d. No one really sees me
- e. I have to be perfect to be safe

2. Where did that sentence come from?
   - a. A person?
   - b. A cultural message?
   - c. A system?
3. How has it shaped your behavior, your relationships, and your self-image?
4. What emotion comes up when you try to speak to yourself with kindness or power?
   - a. Does it feel foreign?
   - b. Awkward?
   - c. Fake?
5. What part of you still doubts it's allowed?
6. What do you fear might happen if you start to believe a new story?

Now Try: Rewriting the Sentence
1. Take the old sentence and gently write a new one.
   Examples:
   - a. I'm not enough → I am already enough, even when I don't feel it.
   - b. If I rest, I'll fail → My rest is part of my strength.
   - c. I'm too much → I am not too much — I am whole.
   - d. I don't belong → I am allowed to exist fully and freely.
2. Say the new sentence out loud.
   - a. How does it feel in your mouth?
   - b. In your chest?
   - c. In your breath?
3. What part of you resists this new sentence — and why?
4. What part of you wants to believe it, even if it's not fully ready?

5. What would it mean to practice this sentence — not as a performance, but as a new rhythm?

Optional Practice: Speak It Into Your Day

Try one of the following:
1. Write your new sentence on a mirror, post-it, or journal
2. Whisper it to yourself when you wake up or before bed
3. Pair it with a breath — inhale truth, exhale fear
4. Share it with someone you trust

This isn't just about words.
It's about voice.
It's about becoming fluent in the language of liberation.
The old sentences were planted in you.
These new ones?
They are yours.

The circle grew quieter for a while. But it isn't silence from fear — it's the kind of silence that comes before something sacred breaks open.

Amara holds up a blank piece of paper.

Amara:
"We've spoken about the words you carry inside. But let's talk now about the way those words show up — not in your mind, but in your body."

The group shifts. Some cross their arms. Some sit straighter.

Grace is the first to speak.

Grace:
"Whenever I tell myself You're not doing enough, my stomach tightens. I stop breathing deeply.
I rush around — like maybe if I just stay busy enough, I won't have to feel it."

81

Malik nods.

Malik:
"When I hear You're too much, my whole body contracts. Like I'm trying to fold myself in half. Even my voice changes. I speak more carefully, like I'm asking permission to exist."

Maria:
"My voice says, You have to earn everything, even kindness. It lands in my shoulders. Like I'm carrying something that isn't mine, but I'm still responsible for it."

Sam:
"I feel it in my chest. That tightness — when I feel like I need to overexplain or justify myself just to be seen as competent. That's class, I think. That's years of trying to sound smart enough to deserve a seat at the table."

Ari:
"And ableism shows up in my jaw. When I try to keep up — even when my brain or body is asking me to pause — I clench. I fake energy I don't have. And inside, the voice is saying: Don't let them see your limits."

Amara speaks softly now.

Amara:
"Internalized oppression is not just cognitive — it is somatic. The voice becomes a posture. A tension. A set of muscles that are always braced for rejection. And if we want to rewrite the script...we must also retrain the body."

They pause, letting it settle.

Amara:

"Let's try something simple. Take the sentence you're working with — the one you're beginning to rewrite. And now say it. But first... unclench. Soften the shoulders. Unfurrow the brow. Breathe into your belly. Say it from your center — not from fear, but from truth."

The group breathes together. A ripple of release fills the room. They speak not loudly, but clearly.

Grace:

"I am doing enough."

Malik:

"My presence does not need permission."

Maria:

"I am allowed to receive, without earning."

Sam:

"I belong here. I always did."

Ari:

"My needs are valid. My limits are sacred."

Amara:

"Yes. This is not just language. This is embodiment. The voice you speak with your body is the one that liberation listens to most."

The circle does not end tonight with heavy silence, but with soft smiles, tentative laughter, and even a shared warmth that wasn't there before.

They have begun to speak again.
This time, in their own voice.

Steps to Awareness

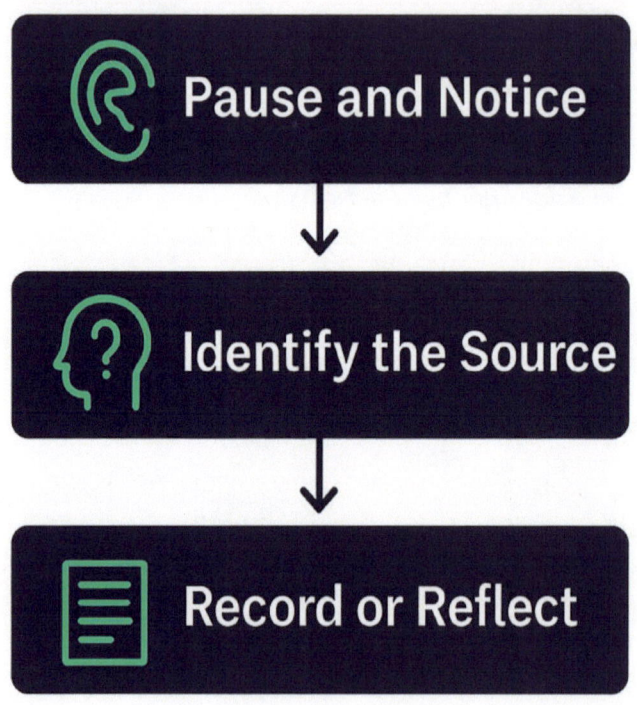

You're beginning to hear yourself

Part III: Tools for Rewriting the Script

Chapter 9 — Awareness: Hearing the Voice You've Been Ignoring

Mindfulness Practices to Tune into Inner Dialogue

Tonight, the circle is quieter, but not with fear — with attention. Everyone has felt the shift from last time. They have begun to hear themselves differently.

Amara lights the candle slowly.

Amara:
"Last time, you found the words you've been saying to yourselves — maybe for years. But what happens when you are not in this circle? When life gets busy? When you forget to listen? Oppression loves silence, but liberation requires awareness. Tonight, we practice hearing the voice — gently, honestly, without judgment."

The group listens carefully.

Ari:
"I don't think I even notice when I talk to myself. It just happens."

Amara:
"That is exactly how oppression stays hidden — through habit. The voice becomes so familiar you stop hearing it. Awareness is what makes it visible. And what becomes visible, can change."

Maria:
"But how do you catch it? It's like breathing. I don't even realize when I'm doing it."

Amara:
"You're right. It happens quietly. But with practice, you will begin to notice. And once you notice, you begin to choose."

Amara places a smooth stone in the center of the circle.

Amara:
"Let's practice.
Close your eyes.
Notice your breath — nothing fancy, just notice.
Now, listen inward.
What is the voice saying — right now?"

Silence. The room seems to slow down.

After a while, Sam speaks softly.

Sam:
"It says I'm taking too long."

Ari half-smiles, nodding.

Maria:
"Mine says, Don't say anything stupid."

Malik:
"Mine says, You're too old for this. You should have figured this out
years ago."

Grace:
"Mine says, You're doing it wrong. Even now."

They all glance at Amara, expecting correction.

Amara:
"Good. You are hearing it. And now you have a choice. You could
continue to believe these voices, Or you could say: Ah, there you are,
old story. I see you."

Ari:
"That's it? Just noticing it?"

Amara:

"At first, yes. Awareness is more powerful than you think. When you become the listener, You are no longer only the one being spoken to. You begin to regain authorship."

The group breathes deeply.

Amara:

"Healing is not always about fixing. Sometimes, it is simply about noticing, kindly."

Sam:

"So, every time I hear the old voice, I just say, I see you?"

Amara:

"Yes. And with time, You will see that you are not the voice — You are the one who hears it. And the one who hears it…Can rewrite it."

Reflection for the Reader: Your First Awareness Practice
For the next 24 hours, simply notice:
1. When does the old voice appear?
2. What does it say?
3. How does your body feel when it shows up?
4. Can you softly say, I see you, without judgment?

Don't try to fix it yet.
Just witness.
Oppression depends on you not noticing.
Liberation begins the moment you do.

Additional Reflection for the Reader: Listening in Real Time
Learning to Catch the Voice as It Speaks — Without Shame,
Without Rush

Awareness is not about control.
It's not about perfection.
It's about presence — coming back to yourself again and again,
especially when it's hard.

Take a breath. Feel your feet. Let's begin.
1. When does the inner voice show up loudest?
    a. When I make a mistake?
    b. When I feel behind, unprepared, or rejected?
    c. When I'm with certain people or in certain spaces?
2. What tone does it use?
    a. Is it harsh? Sarcastic? Anxious? Urgent?
    b. Does it pretend to protect me by keeping me small?
3. What physical sensations accompany it?
4. Tightness in the chest?
    a. Shallow breath?
    b. Tension in the jaw or shoulders?
    c. A heavy stillness or sudden rush?
5. How does my behavior change when I believe the voice?
    a. Do I withdraw?
    b. Do I overperform?
    c. Do I shut down, apologize, or try to prove something?

Now Ask: What Helps Me Hear It — Without Obeying It?
1. What helps me notice the voice while it's happening — not
   hours later?
    a. Slowing my breath?
    b. Naming the emotion?
    c. Pausing before responding?
2. Can I gently say to myself, in the moment:
    a. "There you are, old story. I see you."
    b. "That's the voice — not the truth."
    c. "I don't have to believe that today."

3. What would it look like to treat awareness like a companion, not a correction?
4. What situations do I want to practice awareness in this week?
    a. A meeting?
    b. A family conversation?
    c. A moment of rest or decision-making?

Optional Practice: Awareness Snapshot
For the next 3 days, pause 3 times a day and jot down:
1. What am I thinking right now?
2. What does my body feel like?
3. What is my inner voice saying?
4. Is that voice mine — or inherited?

You are not trying to fix the voice.
You are simply learning to hear it while it speaks, without letting it become your script.

Awareness doesn't always silence the voice —
but it makes space between the voice
and the person you're becoming.

The circle ends tonight not with answers, but with awareness — the quiet power of hearing what has been ignored for too long.
And with awareness comes choice.
And with choice, comes freedom.

INNER OPPRESSOR TOOLBOX

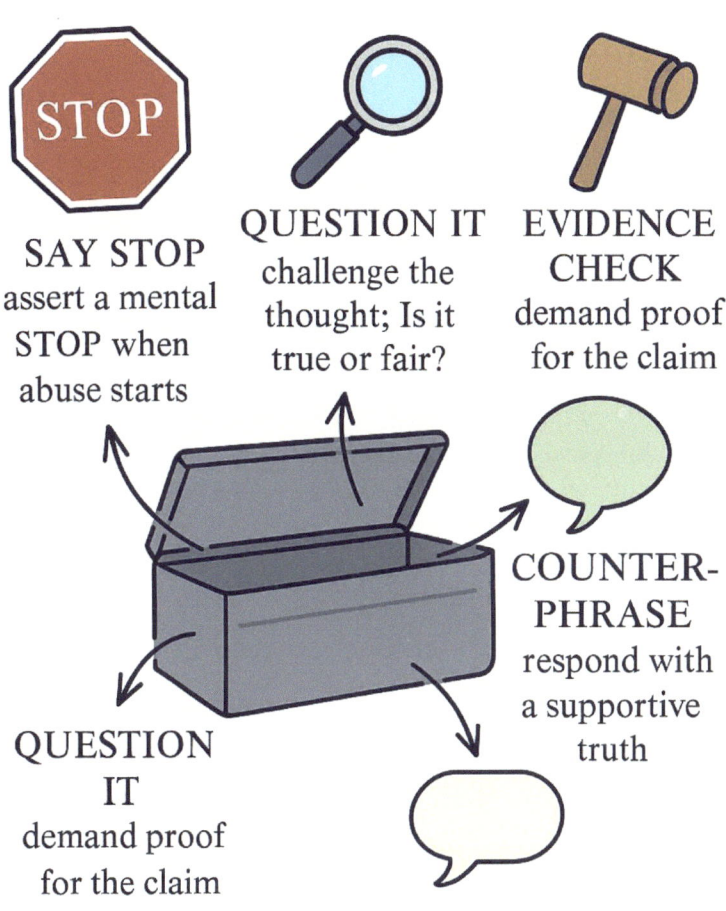

SAY STOP
assert a mental
STOP when
abuse starts

QUESTION IT
challenge the
thought; Is it
true or fair?

EVIDENCE CHECK
demand proof
for the claim

COUNTER-PHRASE
respond with
a supportive
truth

QUESTION IT
demand proof
for the claim

Chapter 10 — Disruption: Interrupting the Inner Oppressor

Courageously Challenging the Old Voice

The circle tonight has a quiet charge. For the first time, the group looks not just ready — but willing. Something is stirring.

Amara enters, carrying a small bowl of water.

Amara:
"Last time, we learned to notice the voice without judgment. Tonight, we take the next step: Disruption."

They dip a hand into the water and let a few drops fall.

Amara:
"Think of oppression as a steady drip — tap, tap, tap — until it carves itself into your mind like stone. The act of noticing slows the drip. But the act of disrupting? That is when you place your hand beneath the water and say: No more."

Maria:
"Disrupting sounds… scary."

Amara:
"It can be. Especially when the voice has lived in you for so long that it feels like home."

Ari:
"How do we disrupt something that feels like us?"

Amara:
*"With kindness. Not by going to war, but by interrupting the pattern. Think of it like this: When you catch the voice saying, I'm not enough, you simply add, **Is that true? Or Says who? Or Thank you for trying to protect me, but I choose a different story now.**"*

92

Sam:
"So, we don't just argue with it?"

Amara:
"Not argue. Question. Questioning is powerful. The voice depends on you not questioning it. It depends on obedience. But you are allowed to interrupt."

Malik:
"But isn't that disrespectful? The voice sometimes sounds like my father, or my mother."

Amara:
"I understand. Many of these voices are borrowed from people we loved. People who were themselves trapped. Disrupting the voice is not dishonoring them — it is liberating them, too. You are not betraying your parents by breaking the pattern. You are freeing them from the silence they were forced to live under."

Maria wipes her eyes.

Maria:
"It's hard to think of it like that. But it makes sense."

Amara:
"Remember: You are not fighting against yourself. You are gently freeing yourself from the parts that were never truly you."

Grace:
"So, the next time I hear the voice say, I should have done more, I can say, I did enough. Or even, Maybe I was never supposed to carry all of this."

Amara:
"Exactly."

Ari:

"And when mine says, You have to be perfect, I can say, I am enough, even imperfect."

Amara smiles.

Amara:

"You are all already speaking the language of disruption."

Sam:

"It feels awkward."

Amara:

"At first, it always does. Oppression taught you fluency in self-criticism. Liberation will feel like learning a new language. But with practice? It will become your native tongue again."

Reflection for the Reader: Disrupt One Sentence
This week, try this:
1. Notice when the old voice appears.
2. Pause and gently ask:
    a. Is that true?
    b. Says who?
    c. Do I want to believe this?
3. Offer a disruption, even if it feels small.

Example:
- **Old Voice**: I'll never belong.
- **Disruption**: Maybe belonging isn't something I have to earn.

Write down one disruption today.

Remember:
You don't have to shout.
A whisper is enough to change the story.

The circle ends with less weight and more curiosity.
They leave not as victims of the voice, but as questioners.
And questioners are dangerous — to oppression.

Additional Reflection for the Reader:
Practicing Disruption — Without Violence, Without Shame

Creating Space Between the Voice and Your Truth
Disruption doesn't have to be loud.
It doesn't have to be angry.
It only has to be clear.

You don't have to destroy the voice.
You only need to stop obeying it.

Take a breath — in through the nose, slow.
Out through the mouth, softer still.
Let's begin.

1. Think of a moment recently when the old voice showed up.
   a. What did it say?
   b. What did it expect you to do?
   c. How did your body respond?

2. In that moment — or a future one — what might disruption look like?
   Here are options. Which ones feel like they belong to you?
   Disruption with Language
   - Saying aloud: That's not my truth anymore.
   - Whispering: That's an old script. I don't have to follow it.
   - Asking: Is that even true? Says who?
   Disruption with Breath
   - Pausing for a single, intentional breath
   - Exhaling the voice out of your body
   - Using your breath to ground before responding, choosing, or speaking

Disruption with the Body
- Unclenching your jaw or fists
- Uncrossing your arms
- Sitting back in your chair with softness
- Standing or walking with your full presence — reclaiming space
- Smiling, frowning, shaking — doing anything that makes the moment yours again
  Disruption with Choice
- Saying no
- Not explaining
- Resting when guilt says work
- Speaking when fear says be silent
- Leaving when history says stay

3. What gets in the way of disrupting the voice?
   a. Fear of backlash?
   b. Fear of being seen?
   c. Fear of failure or rejection?

4. What would help you feel safe enough to disrupt, even just a little?

5. What is your own language for disruption — one that sounds like you?

Optional Practice: Write Your Disruption Self-Affirming Statement
Complete the sentence:

When the old voice says _____,
I now respond with _____.

Repeat it daily. Say it with your breath.
Say it to your mirror.
Say it to your inner child.

Let the disruption become your freedom song.

You are not fighting the voice.
You are freeing yourself from its grip.

Disruption is not about rage.
It is about reclaiming authorship — sentence by sentence.

Chapter 11 — Replacement: Planting the Seeds of Self-Liberation

Creating New Inner Language Rooted in Truth and Dignity

GROWTH JOURNEY
Planting the Seeds of Self-Liberation

| New Empowering Belief or Affirmation | First Sprout trying out the new belief tentatively | Nurture reinforcing through practice and support | Flourishing Self-Worth the new narrative solidifies |

There is a stillness in the circle tonight, but not from silence. It's the stillness of fertile soil, turned over, ready for something new.

Amara places a small bag of seeds on the table in front of them.

Amara:
"We've spent time naming the voice. Noticing it. Interrupting it. Now, we plant something new."

The circle leans in.

Amara:
"Imagine the mind as a field. For years, it has grown whatever was planted — fear, self-doubt, shame. Not because of who you are, but because of what was sown. Tonight, we plant on purpose."

Maria speaks first, slowly.

Maria:
"If I've always said, I have to earn rest, what do I plant instead?"

Amara:
"You might plant. Rest is not earned. It is part of being alive. Or I am allowed to receive as much as I give. The words don't have to be perfect. They just have to be true."

Ari:
"Mine says, You're only valuable when you achieve. I guess I could say, my value is not measured by productivity. But it doesn't feel true yet."

Amara:
"That's okay. The soil does not reject the seed just because it takes time to sprout. Say it anyway. Water it anyway."

Sam:
"My old voice says, You're too much. I want to plant, my presence is not too much. It's medicine."

Malik smiles for the first time all evening.

Malik:
"Mine has always said, Don't expect too much. Play it safe. But I want to say, I am allowed to want more. I am allowed to grow."

Grace speaks quietly.

Grace:
"My voice says, You should've done more. But I want to say, I am enough, and I am still learning."

The group looks at each other, moved — not by perfection, but by possibility.

Amara:

"These are your new truths. Not fantasies. Not toxic positivity. But the remembering of what has always been real, beneath the noise. Say them. Write them. Repeat them. Let them take root."

Reflection for the Reader: Write Your New Script
Take a quiet moment.
1. What is one old sentence you have lived by?
2. Now, write a new sentence to plant in its place.
It does not need to feel fully believable yet.
It only needs to be rooted in your deeper truth.

Old Script:

_____
_____
_____
_____
_____

New Script:

_____
_____
_____
_____
_____

Say it aloud.
Whisper it.
Write it on your mirror.
Breathe it into your day.
You are not faking it.
You are planting it.
And with time, it will bloom.

Tonight, the circle ends with everyone writing — not about who they were, but who they are becoming.

The air smells like earth and hope.
The stories are changing.
And the soil is ready.

Additional Reflection for the Reader: Choosing Your New Language
Letting Go of Scripts That Were Never Yours — and Planting the
Words You Were Meant to Speak

This is not about perfect affirmations.
It's about truth.
It's about language that your body, your spirit, and your future self can
begin to trust.

Take a slow breath. Feel your feet.
Let your old voice rise — without fear.
And now let's begin to rewrite it.

1. What sentence — or belief — am I ready to stop rehearsing?
   Examples:
   a. I have to earn my worth.
   b. I'm too broken to be loved.
   c. If I rest, I fall behind.
   d. I'm not smart, beautiful, strong, disciplined, or good
      enough.
   e. Someone like me doesn't get to ask for more.
2. Where did this sentence come from?
   a. A person?
   b. A community?
   c. A system?
   d. A survival strategy?
3. How does this sentence make me feel — in my body, my
   spirit, my relationships?
4. What might it look like to speak back to it — not with denial,
   but with liberation?

Now: Begin to Plant Something New
1. What sentence do I want to plant in its place?

101

Options to try:
- a. I am already enough.
- b. My presence is not a problem.
- c. I am allowed to receive care and still be strong.
- d. My needs are valid. My voice matters.
- e. I am not too much. I am whole.
- f. I don't need to suffer to deserve rest.

2. Say it out loud — even if it feels awkward or fake.
   - a. What part of you wants to believe it?
   - b. What part of you resists it?
3. How does your body respond when you say the new sentence?
   - a. Do you soften?
   - b. Do you brace?
   - c. Do you cry?
   - d. Do you feel still?
4. What does your younger self — or your future self — want to hear from you today?

Optional Practice: The Planting Ritual
1. Write your new sentence on a slip of paper.
2. Place it somewhere visible — a mirror, a phone screen, a pocket.
3. Every day this week, speak it to yourself with your hand on your heart or belly.
4. Say it when you wake up. Say it when the old voice tries to take over. Say it before you sleep.

You are not pretending.
You are planting.

This new voice may feel unfamiliar.
But unfamiliar does not mean untrue.

You are not erasing who you've been.
You are remembering who you've always been — before the world told you otherwise.

Notes:

In this chapter:

- We emphasize replacement not as fake optimism, but truth-reclamation.
- Each character shows how planting new language can be gentle, imperfect, and real.
- We prepare you, the reader, for Chapter 12, where repetition becomes a path to inner fluency.

Chapter 12 — Repetition: Becoming Fluent in Self-Worth

How to Make Healing Sustainable

The circle is glowing tonight. Not just from the candle, but from the people gathered. Something is different. Something is growing.

Amara waits for a while before speaking.

Amara:
"How do you learn a language? How do you become fluent? By speaking it — again and again — even when it feels awkward."

Maria:
"So, you mean, just keep saying the new sentence until it feels natural?"

Amara:
"Exactly. But not like a punishment. Not like forcing yourself. Like watering a plant. Like singing a song. Like remembering a melody you once knew by heart."

Sam:
"But what about the old voice? It's still there. Even after all this."

Amara:
"It will be. The old voice is like a path you have walked a thousand times. It's familiar, well-worn. The new voice? It's the new path, still soft, still growing. At first, you will forget. You will default. And that's okay. But every time you choose the new sentence — even one time — you strengthen it."

Malik:
"So, it's not about getting it perfect?"

Amara:
"No. It's about practicing. Liberation is not a moment. It's a rhythm. And rhythms are learned by repeating."

Ari:
"What if we fall back into the old voice? Like, a bad day happens and I hear, You're failing. You're not enough. Loud and clear."

Amara:
"That's not failure. That is life. The question is not, Did the voice return? The question is, Did you notice? And if you noticed, you have already disrupted it."

The circle is still.

Amara:
"With time, the new voice becomes louder. Not by magic. But by practice. By showing up to yourself every day, even when it feels strange."

Grace:
"So healing is not just about understanding. It's about repetition."

Amara:
"Exactly. Not as punishment. But as devotion. You are learning the language of liberation — one word, one breath, one choice at a time."

Reflection for the Reader: Build Your Rhythm
Take a few breaths.

Choose one new sentence you planted.
- Can you repeat it each morning?
- Can you write it somewhere visible?
- Can you whisper it when the old voice appears?

Remember:
You are not faking it.
You are practicing.

Liberation is learned,
not inherited.

The circle closes tonight, not with urgency, but with commitment.
They are no longer searching for the path —
they are walking it,
one quiet, repeated step at a time.

Additional Reflection for the Reader: Practicing Until It Becomes Your Voice
Building Inner Fluency in Self-Worth, One Gentle Repetition at a Time

Staircase of Fluency

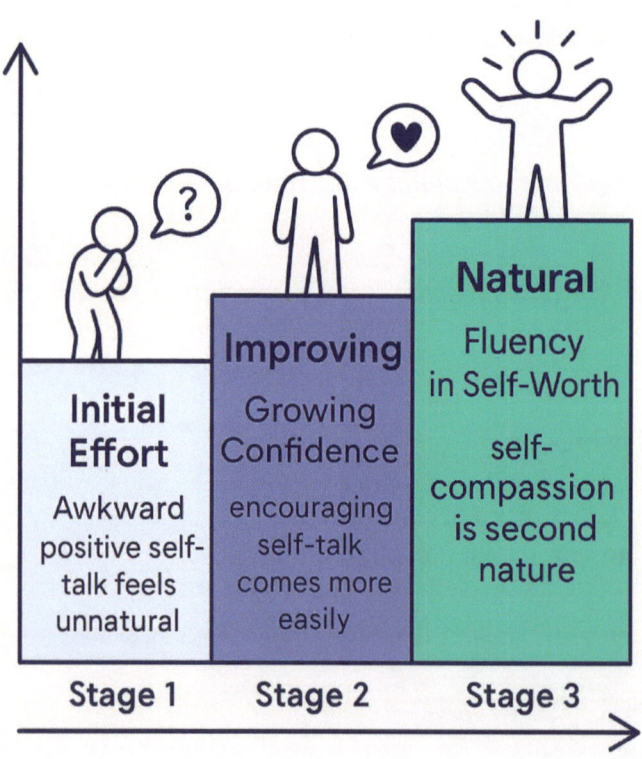

| Stage 1 | Stage 2 | Stage 3 |

You are not repeating to convince yourself.
You are repeating to remember.

Healing isn't about finding the perfect words once.
It's about choosing the true ones again and again
— until they sound like home.

Take a breath. Let's begin.
1. What is the new sentence I've chosen to speak to myself?
2. Write it again here. Say it aloud.
3. When does this sentence feel believable?
    a. After rest?
    b. In solitude?
    c. When I'm with people who see me clearly?
4. When does this sentence feel out of reach?
    a. During conflict?
    b. When I make mistakes?
    c. When I'm triggered or exhausted?
5. How do I tend to judge myself for not believing the new voice right away?

Now Ask: What If Practice Is the Point?
1. What would it look like to treat repetition like brushing your teeth, not like passing a test?
2. Where can I embed this new language into my daily rhythm? Ideas:
    a. On a mirror
    b. As a phone reminder
    c. In a journal
    d. Spoken during handwashing, walking, or breathwork
    e. Repeated silently while in line, on the train, or in stressful moments
3. Can I pair my new sentence with a simple body cue?
    a. A deep breath
    b. A hand over heart or belly
    c. An exhale with intention
    d. A posture of dignity

4. What wouldn't it mean if I forgot the sentence some days?
   a. It wouldn't mean I've failed.
   b. It wouldn't mean the old voice won.
   c. It wouldn't mean I'm not healing.
5. What would it mean to begin again, without shame?

Optional Practice: Build a Repetition Ritual
Create a 30-second daily ritual:
1. Name the sentence
2. Breathe with the sentence
3. Move with the sentence (stretch, soften, stand)
4. Close with gratitude — even just one hand over your heart

Example:
I am already enough.
(Inhale)
I am already enough.
(Exhale)
(Stand tall or soften shoulders)
Thank you, body, for remembering.

Repeat this once a day. Let it become your rhythm.
Repetition is not punishment.
It is devotion.
It is remembrance.

Every time you choose the new sentence,
you strengthen the path home.

You are not becoming someone new.
You are becoming fluent in your truth.

Part IV: From Personal Healing to Collective Power

Chapter 13 — Reclaiming Space and Voice

Showing Up in the World with Unapologetic Presence

Tonight, the circle feels both tender and electric. The weeks have softened them, but they also sit taller. Even in their silence, they take up more space.

Amara lights the candle and, for the first time, stands.

Amara:
"You have done the hard work. You have seen the voice. You have disrupted it. You have planted something new. Now comes the next step — reclaiming space, and letting the world hear your true voice."

The group shifts. This feels bigger, somehow.

Maria:
"But isn't that dangerous? I've spent my whole life trying not to take up space. To stay small. To be grateful, quiet, helpful."

Amara:
"Dangerous? Sometimes, yes. But costly? Always. What is the cost of staying small? What have you lost by shrinking?"

Maria wipes a tear away but says nothing.

Ari:
"I don't even know who I am without shrinking. At work, I perform. At home, I perform. Even here, sometimes. How do I even begin to show up differently?"

Amara:
"You don't have to tear down the walls all at once. Reclaiming space is not always a roar. Sometimes, it is a whisper. Sometimes, it is choosing to speak when you would have stayed silent. Sometimes, it is saying no. Sometimes, it is saying yes when fear says hide."

Sam:
"And when people don't like it? When they look at you like you've broken some unspoken rule?"

Amara:
"Then you know you are practicing liberation. Oppression is designed to make you fear taking up space. Liberation is learning that the discomfort of others is not the measure of your worth."

Malik:
"I still hear the old voice — Play it safe. Don't draw attention. And to be honest, sometimes I listen."

Amara:
"That is okay. This is not about being fearless. It is about being faithful — faithful to yourself. Faithful to the small voice that says, Maybe I am allowed to live fully, even if the world is not ready."

Grace:
"I think I've been hiding behind being 'the helper.' It's easier to advocate for others than to show up fully for myself."

Amara:
"Many of us do that. But remember: Your presence is not a problem to solve. It is a gift to offer. Showing up fully — in voice, in body, in truth — is how we begin to teach the world a different story."

The group sits with this.
No one rushes to speak.

Amara:
"This is the shift — healing is not only inward. It is how you live. How you take up space. How you dare to belong without apology."

Reflection for the Reader: What Would Reclaiming Space Look Like for You?

111

Ask yourself:
1. Where in your life have you stayed small, quiet, or hidden?
2. What might it look like to take up a little more space?
3. To say no.
4. To say yes.
5. To show up as you are.

Write it down.
Be specific.
You do not have to reclaim everything today.
You only have to begin.
And you do not have to ask for permission.

The circle does not close with finality, but with readiness.
Some sit taller.
Some breathe deeper.
Some even laugh.
They are no longer just surviving the story.
They are beginning to write it.

Additional Reflection for the Reader: Taking Up Space Without Asking Permission
Exploring What It Means to Show Up Fully — In Voice, Body, and Truth

You are not too much.
You are not a burden.
You do not have to shrink to be loved, included, or safe.

This chapter invites you to ask:
What does it look like to stop asking for permission to exist?

1. In what areas of my life have I learned to shrink?
   Examples:
   a. At work (withholding my ideas, minimizing my strengths)
   b. In family (silencing opinions, over-functioning, being the peacekeeper)

c. In public spaces (making myself invisible or less expressive)
d. In relationships (apologizing for my emotions, needs, or boundaries)
e. In my body (changing posture, tone, or expression to appear "smaller")
2. Where did I learn that shrinking = safety, likability, or success?
3. What does reclaiming space look like to me — emotionally, physically, energetically?
4. What are the smallest spaces I occupy — and what does it feel like to stretch them, even slightly?

Now Ask: What Would It Mean to Take Up Space With Dignity?
1. How would I walk if I weren't afraid to be seen?
2. What would my voice sound like if I weren't trying to manage how others feel?
3. What would I say — or stop saying — if I believed I didn't have to apologize for my truth?
4. How would I dress, speak, move, or rest if I trusted that I belong here?
5. What part of me still believes that shrinking is safer than being seen — and what part of me is ready for something different?

Optional Practice: Space Reclamation Ritual
Today or this week, try one of the following:
1. Sit or stand without crossing your arms, tucking your feet, or leaning away
2. Speak up in a space where you normally stay quiet — even just once
3. Say no or yes without justification
4. Wear something that makes you feel present, powerful, or unhidden
5. Take a deep breath in a public space, and exhale without apology
6. Take a longer pause before responding — and let your silence carry weight

Write or whisper this sentence:
I am allowed to be here. I do not need to shrink to be safe.

You don't need to dominate to reclaim space.
You only need to stop abandoning yourself.
The more space you take up,
the more you remind the world — and yourself — that presence is
not a threat.
It is your return.

Chapter 14 — Circles of Healing: Community as Catalyst

How Collective Reflection Supports Inner Transformation

Tonight, the circle arrives differently.

There is a softness, but also a quiet strength in the way they greet each other. Shoulders rest easier. The silence feels like connection, not avoidance.

Amara watches them carefully before speaking.

Amara:
"What happens when you no longer try to do this alone?"

The group glances at each other.

Ari:
"You stop feeling like the problem."

Sam:
"You realize… it wasn't just you all along."

Amara:
"Exactly. Liberation is not designed to be done in isolation. Oppression isolates. But healing, real healing — thrives in community."

Amara looks around the room.

Amara:
"Every time you spoke here — you healed. Every time you listened — you healed. Every time you saw yourself in another — you remembered you weren't alone."

Maria:
"I spent so many years believing that my silence was just my issue. That it was about me. But here, hearing all of you... I realized — it's a system. It's history. It's bigger than me.
And yet, it can be undone."

Malik:
"When I heard Ari say I have to be perfect, I saw myself. When Sam said I'm too much, I felt it in my chest. Turns out, I wasn't carrying my own burden alone. We've all been walking around with the same story — just in different languages."

Grace:
"And when Maria named her exhaustion, it gave me permission to name mine."

Amara smiles.

Amara:
"This is why we sit in circle. This is why oppressed people have always gathered — around kitchen tables, in church basements, in quiet corners, in marches and vigils. Not just to mourn. Not just to survive. But to remember together. To unlearn together. To rebuild together."

Sam:
"But what if you don't have a circle like this outside of here? What if your community is stuck, too?"

Amara:
"Then you build it, slowly. One conversation. One relationship. One honest moment at a time."

Ari:
"What if no one wants to listen?"

Amara:
"Someone always will. And sometimes, the first person you must invite into the circle is yourself."

The group falls into silence, this time filled with possibility.

Amara:
"You are living proof that we heal faster, deeper, and more sustainably when we do it together. Liberation is not just personal — it is relational."

Reflection for the Reader: Who is in Your Circle?
Ask yourself:
- Who are the people who listen to you?
- Who are the people you can speak honestly with?
- Who are the people you might invite into this kind of conversation — gently, without expectation?

If you don't have them yet,
start by becoming that person for someone else.
You do not have to heal alone.
In fact, you were never meant to.

Tonight, the circle does not end with answers, but with a simple, quiet truth:
They are no longer just individuals doing the work.
They are a circle.
They are a movement.
They are home.

Additional Reflection for the Reader: Who Are You Healing With?
Exploring the People, Spaces, and Circles That Shape Your Voice

Liberation may begin within — but it deepens in connection. Healing accelerates when we are seen, heard, and held in our wholeness.

Let's explore your healing ecosystem — the people and spaces you are (or aren't) doing this work with.

1. Who in my life allows me to show up without performance, apology, or pretense?
2. Who makes space for my voice, even when it trembles — or especially when it trembles?
3. Who models a relationship with themselves that feels liberating to witness?
4. What spaces in my life (circles, friendships, communities, teams) feel like they are built on trust, truth, and dignity?
5. Where do I still feel the need to:
   a. Code-switch
   b. Shrink
   c. Manage others' comfort
   d. Prove myself
   e. Hide my pain or joy
   f. Avoid vulnerability?
6. What is the emotional cost of staying in those spaces — or keeping certain relationships unchanged?

Now Ask: How Can I Co-Create Liberating Community?
1. What does a healing circle mean to me?
   a. It could be literal (a group or gathering)
   b. Or metaphorical (a relationship, an agreement, a rhythm)
2. What qualities do I want in the people I heal with?
   a. Gentleness?
   b. Accountability?
   c. Humor?
   d. Shared values?
3. What do I bring to a healing circle?
   a. Wisdom?
   b. Deep listening?
   c. Honesty?
   d. Experience?
   e. Creative ways of holding space?
4. What might I need to grieve or release in order to find or build that kind of community?
5. Who could I reach out to — today — to begin practicing more honest, liberating connection?

Optional Practice: Map Your Circle
On a blank page, draw yourself at the center.
- Around you, name the people who hold you in your healing.
- Use closer or wider circles to reflect your current connection.
- Add who you wish to call in, or what qualities you are seeking.

This is not about perfection.
It's about intention.
You are allowed to create the community your soul has been waiting for.
Your healing is magnified in community.
Your voice grows louder when it echoes with others.
You are not meant to do this alone.
You are already a circle.
And somewhere, someone is waiting to sit in it with you.

Chapter 15 — Parenting, Mentoring, and Modeling New Narratives

Creating Legacies of Healing, Pride, and Power

The circle is quieter tonight, but not with heaviness — with reflection. As if each person knows they are standing on the edge of something larger than themselves.

Amara leans forward, resting their hands on their knees.

Amara:
"You have begun to rewrite your story. Now, we ask — what story will you pass on?"

The question lingers.
Maria speaks first.

Maria:
"I see it every day with my son. The things I say to myself, sometimes I say to him without realizing it. I tell him not to make trouble. Not to ask for too much. To be grateful. And I hear my mother's voice come out of my mouth."

Her voice trembles.

Maria:
"I love him more than anything. And still, I pass it on."

Ari nods.

Ari:
"I do it too. I mentor younger folks at work, and I realize I sometimes encourage them to overwork, to be twice as good, because that's what I thought I had to do to survive."

Malik:
"I've told kids, Don't hope too much.

Not because I wanted to steal their dreams,
but because I was trying to protect them."

Amara:
"You have all named the pattern. And by naming it, you are already interrupting it. You are not doomed to repeat it."

Sam:
"But we inherited it. And so did they. It feels too deep to undo."

Amara:
"Deep, yes. But not permanent. Patterns are powerful, but they are still just patterns. And patterns can be broken."

Grace:
"How?"

Amara:
"By modeling. By living differently, even when it feels unfamiliar. When you rest without guilt, when you speak without apology, when you love yourself out loud, you give others permission to do the same."

Maria:
"So, we teach, not just with words — but with how we live."

Amara:
"Exactly. Children notice when we rest, when we set boundaries, when we tell ourselves a kinder story. Clients notice. Students notice. Neighbors notice. And most importantly — you notice."

The circle falls into a quiet knowing.

Amara:
"Your healing is not just for you. It is for everyone who watches you. For everyone who follows you. For everyone who was waiting for permission to heal."

Malik:
"Maybe we don't need to save them. Maybe we just need to live differently so, they know it's possible."

Amara:
"Exactly."

Reflection for the Reader: Who Are You Modeling For?
1. Who watches you?
    a. Children?
    b. Students?
    c. Clients?
    d. Younger versions of yourself?
2. What do they see?
3. What would it mean if they saw you
    a. Rest
    b. Say no kindly
    c. Speak your truth
    d. Believe you are enough

You do not have to teach by lecturing.
You teach by living.
And you are already teaching.
Tonight, the circle closes with no rush to leave.
They sit for a while longer,
each quietly realizing that healing is never just personal.
It is always,
always,
generational.

Reflection for the Reader: What Are You Passing On?
Choosing to Model Liberation Instead of Inheriting Oppression

You are not responsible for the pain you inherited.
But you are powerful enough to choose what grows from here.

This chapter invites you to pause and ask:
What story am I modeling — and what story do I want to pass on?

1. Think of a person you care for, support, or influence.
    a. A child.
    b. A student.
    c. A client.
    d. A friend.
    e. A younger version of yourself.
2. What messages are they receiving — spoken or unspoken — by how you treat yourself in front of them?

Examples:
    a. How you talk about your body, rest, worth, time, or boundaries
    b. How you handle failure, silence, or joy
    c. How you respond to your own needs or emotions
3. What old narratives do you hear yourself repeating, even though you never meant to?
4. What part of you is still operating from an inherited script — even when you're trying to help or protect others?

Now Ask: What Would It Look Like to Model Something New?
1. What would it look like to show others — especially younger people — what freedom sounds like?
2. What do I want the next generation to believe about:
    a. Their worth?
    b. Their voice?
    c. Their right to rest, belong, heal, and dream?
3. What does modeling look like for me?
    a. Do I need to speak more clearly?
    b. Soften more intentionally?
    c. Set more loving boundaries?
    d. Let myself be seen?
4. What does imperfection in modeling look like — and how can I embrace it without shame?
5. What might change if I trusted that my own healing gives others permission to begin theirs?

Optional Practice: Legacy Letter

Write a short note (to a child, mentee, client, younger version of yourself, or a future ancestor). Complete the sentences below or make your own.

1. Here's what I believed once, but no longer do:
2. Here's what I want you to know about your voice:
3. Here's what I hope you inherit from me:
4. Here's what ends with me — and doesn't get passed on:

Let your letter be an offering.
You are not only healing yourself.
You are shifting the future.
Healing isn't always what you say.
Sometimes it's how you stand.
Sometimes it's how you rest.
Sometimes it's the sentence you no longer speak aloud —
because you've stopped believing it inside.
You are modeling something sacred.
You are not repeating the cycle.
You are rewriting it.

Chapter 16 — Liberation is Contagious

How Your Healing Transforms Families, Systems, and Society

The circle gathers for what they all know is the last formal meeting. The candlelight feels different tonight — not softer, but brighter. No one speaks at first, until Amara finally breaks the silence.

Amara:
"What if I told you that you've already begun the revolution?"

Sam looks surprised.

Sam:
"But nothing's changed out there."

Amara:
"Hasn't it? Isn't it true that you hear the voice differently now? That you pause before you speak to yourself? That you've remembered you have a choice?"

The group nods, slowly.

Amara:
"And don't you think the world feels that, even if they don't know what they're feeling? Doesn't your child notice? Your colleague? Your neighbor? The stranger on the street who sees you stand just a little taller?"

Maria:
"So, this… spreads?"

Amara:
"Of course it spreads. Liberation is contagious."

Malik:
"But what about the systems? The racism, the poverty, the injustice — they're still out there."

Amara:
"Yes. And they will not crumble overnight. But systems are upheld by people — and people carry stories inside them. Every time one person reclaims their voice, their worth,
their breath — the system loses a little of its grip."

Grace:
"So, healing isn't a retreat from the world — it's how we change it."

Amara:
"Exactly. What if the greatest resistance is not only what you march for, but who you become? What if every act of self-compassion is a brick removed from the wall? What if every time you refuse to abandon yourself, you teach the world a new possibility?"

The group sits still, taking it in.

Ari:
"I always thought the revolution was out there. But maybe it starts here."

Amara:
"It always has. The systems that shaped your inner world were external, yes — but the undoing of them — the re-claiming — begins right here."

Amara points gently to each of them.

Amara:
"And then here." (Points to the circle.)

Amara:
"And then here." (Points beyond the walls.)

Sam:
"So, the revolution starts within, but it doesn't end there."

Amara:
"It can't. It was never meant to. You are allowed to bring your healing into your work, your parenting, your art, your organizing, your silence, your joy. Liberation is not a destination. It is a way of being. And every time you practice it — it ripples."

The candle flickers brightly, as if in agreement.

Maria:
"So, this is not just about me."

Amara:
"It never was."

The circle breathes deeply.
For the first time, they are not just witnessing the revolution.
They are it.

Reflection for the Reader: Your Ripple
Ask yourself:
1. What will you do differently now?
2. How will you walk through the world with your new story?
3. What small act of liberation can you model today —
   a. for yourself,
   b. for someone watching,
   c. for someone who might never tell you they were watching?

Write it down.
And remember:
- The revolution begins within.
- But it never stays there.
- The circle does not formally end.
- They simply sit together —
  o no one smaller,
  o no one silenced,
  o no one alone.

- The story is still being written.
- And so is yours.

Additional Reflection for the Reader: How Are You Changing the World Without Even Knowing It?
Recognizing the Ripple Effect of Your Inner Work

You've done something brave.
You've listened.
You've remembered.
You've rewritten.

Now, ask yourself:
1. How is the world already different — because I am showing up differently?
2. What am I no longer believing — or obeying — that I once thought was truth?
3. What have I reclaimed in the last chapters?
   a. My voice?
   b. My rest?
   c. My boundaries?
   d. My softness?
   e. My space?
4. Who has already felt the shift in me — even if I haven't told them what's happening?
5. What new conversations have I started — even silently — just by being more present, honest, or whole?
6. What systems, roles, or expectations no longer have the same hold on me?
7. What version of myself have I released?
8. What version am I stepping into now?

Now Ask: What Is the World Learning From Me?
1. Who is watching me live differently?
   a. A child?
   b. A friend?
   c. A coworker?

2. Someone I'll never meet — but who feels the ripple?
3. What if my joy, my rest, my refusal to perform — is teaching others what's possible?
4. What would it look like to trust that my personal healing is an act of collective defiance?
5. What would it mean to walk forward — not perfectly, but consistently — as someone who models liberation?

Optional Practice: Your Liberation Ripple
On a blank page, draw three circles.
- In the center, write: How I'm showing up differently
- In the next ring, write: How that affects people closest to me
- In the outer ring, write: How that might ripple into the world — even if I never see it

Write this sentence to close:
- I am living the revolution from the inside out.
- My healing is contagious. My presence is powerful.
- I am not alone, and I never have been.

This is not the end of your story.
It's the beginning of your movement.
Your healing is not quiet.
It is resonant.
It touches spaces far beyond your knowing.
You are already making the world more possible —
just by being more fully yourself.

Summary: What Makes Liberation Possible — Now

You've come far.

You began with a voice in your head — one you didn't choose, but one you had lived with for so long it felt like yours.

You heard it in moments of shame, fear, pressure, or silence.
You traced it back — to parents, teachers, systems, media, society.
You saw how race, gender, class, body, ability, and silence shaped it.
You named it.
You sat with it.
You grieved it.
You spoke back.

You watched it live in your body — in your shoulders, your jaw, your pace, your posture.
You softened where you had learned to clench.
You breathed where you had forgotten how.

You practiced noticing — in the middle of life, not just in stillness.
You disrupted — not with violence, but with clarity.
You replaced — not with slogans, but with sentences rooted in truth.

You repeated.
You stumbled.
You forgot.
You returned.

And slowly, you began to speak to yourself in a new voice.
Not louder.
But real.
Not perfect.
But yours.

You took up more space.
You rested without apology.
You stopped asking for permission to be whole.
You remembered that your healing does not make you selfish — it makes you contagious.

You looked at your community.
You saw who held you and who silenced you.
You grieved what had to be released.
You began building new circles — even if they started with just one other soul.

You looked at those you mentor, parent, teach, or support.
And you chose to stop the cycle.
You chose to model presence instead of perfection.
Wholeness instead of performance.
Joy instead of justification.

And now, here you are.

Still learning.
Still becoming.
Still choosing — every day — to believe a little more in the truth of who you are.

What makes it possible now?

You've done the work.
You've remembered what was never broken.
You've rewritten the script — line by line, breath by breath.

And now, you are no longer the character trapped in someone else's story.
You are the author.
And the page is yours.

Epilogue: You Were Always the Author

There is a moment — quiet, unmistakable — when the voice that once whispered your unworthiness goes silent, not because it has disappeared, but because you no longer believe it.

You've done something revolutionary, you've questioned the unquestioned, you've named the inherited, you've interrupted the story, and now, you are writing a new one, not a perfect story, not a story without grief or questions, but a true one, one rooted in your dignity, one shaped by your remembering, and one that cannot be undone.

You were never broken, only buried, beneath the scripts and roles, beneath the silence and survival, beneath the shame that was never yours to carry.

What you are now reclaiming is not new; rather, it is original, it is yours, it is the voice that was always there — waiting to be heard.

As such, this is not the end, this is the turning point, and from here, your voice carries into every space you enter, and it reshapes your relationships, your leadership, and your lineage.

From here, you pass down something new, not just survival, not just strength, but wholeness, truth, and the freedom to speak, dream, and rest, without apology.

Dear Friend,
You are not just healing yourself, you are healing the future. Let the old script then end with you. Let the new one begin —with love, with courage, and with your name written in every line.

Conclusion — You Are the Author Now

A Final Reflection on Courage, Transformation, and Rewriting the Future

There is no candle tonight, no circle in the room, but you are still here, and that means the circle never ended; rather, it simply changed form.

You have sat with the voices, you have named them, you have questioned them, you have disrupted them, and you have planted new words, watered them with attention, and begun the rhythm of remembrance.

Now, you are the author, you are no longer only the character living inside a story written by systems you did not choose; rather, you are the storyteller, the one who gets to say:

This is who I am now. This is how I speak to myself now. This is how I show up. This is how I resist.

You are now the one who gets to say: This is how I love. This is how I teach. This is how I live, and this is how I liberate — inside and out.

The circle you read about is no longer confined to these pages; rather, it is already inside you. Every time you notice your voice, every time you choose a new word, every time you offer yourself kindness instead of criticism, and every time you choose to rest, to speak, to hope, or to love without shrinking, you are writing.

Further, you are not writing alone, you are joining the millions who, quietly or loudly, are refusing to obey the old scripts. You are joining the movement of people who are choosing liberation, not only for themselves, but for all those watching, listening, following, and dreaming beside them.

Remember:
Your healing is not selfish, your joy is not indulgent, and your voice is not too much. Moreover, your breath is not borrowed, your space is not stolen; rather, it is yours, you are allowed to be here fully, wholly, and unapologetically.

As such, every time you take up that space, whether in words, in silence, in laughter, in tears,
you are teaching the world to remember, too.

So go, write, live, and breathe. For the revolution is already happening, and you are part of it.

Invitation to You, the Reader

Reflection

Now that you've journeyed through these pages,
we invite you to pause… to breathe… and to ask yourself:

What voice are you no longer willing to believe?
What new truth are you ready to live into — out loud?
What legacy will your inner dialogue now pass on?

Take time. Revisit any page. Gather your thoughts in a journal.
Or share them in conversation, in circle, in community.

Your voice matters. Your transformation matters. And your story is
far from over.

Call to Action

Liberation doesn't happen in isolation.
If this book spoke to something inside you —If it helped you see
yourself or others more clearly —If it gave you tools, language, or
hope —Please share it.
With your circle.
With your clients.
With your family.
With those still searching for a way to begin.

Let this book ripple.

Leave a Reflection. Leave a Review.

Books like this travel by word of mouth, heart to heart.

If this journey meant something to you, please take one minute to leave
a review — on Amazon, Goodreads, or wherever you found this book.

Your reflection could be the very reason someone else chooses to begin their healing. Your words can help another reader say, "Maybe it's time I rewrite my script too."

Thank you for walking this path with us.
Now, pass it on.

Reader Integration Toolkit

This book is not meant to be passively read. It's designed to be lived. Healing internalized oppression requires not just insight — but integration. Use this toolkit to begin applying what you've read, in real time, with compassion, courage, and consistency.

The 4-Step Inner Liberation Practice
Use this as your foundational practice — daily, weekly, or whenever you're activated:
Step 1: Awareness – Hear the Voice
- "What am I saying to myself right now?"
- Name the tone, the words, the message.
- Is it limiting? Shaming? Dismissive?

Step 2: Disruption – Interrupt the Oppressor's Voice
- "Where did this voice come from?"
- Challenge its origin. Speak back — with truth, not self-attack.

Step 3: Replacement – Speak a Liberating Truth
- "What would I say to someone I love in this moment?"
- Speak to yourself with dignity, kindness, and grounded honesty.

Step 4: Repetition – Reinforce the New Narrative
- "How can I rehearse this truth today?"
- Use journaling, mirror work, reminders, or rituals to solidify new self-talk.

Daily Self-Affirming Statements
Choose 1–3 each morning. Say them out loud, write them down, and revisit them throughout your day.
- I am not the voice of oppression inside me. I am the one who chooses the script.
- I am allowed to rest, to dream, to take up space, and to be imperfect.
- My voice matters — even when it shakes.
- I do not have to earn my worth. I already am enough.
- I unlearn what harms. I remember what heals.
- Every time I speak to myself with love, I disrupt oppression.

Inner Dialogue Journaling Prompts

Use these for weekly reflection or healing circles:

- What inner script did I inherit, and how has it shaped me?
- When do I shrink, hide, or overperform to feel "safe"?
- What would it mean to be fully, unapologetically myself?
- Whose voice do I still carry — and who would I be without it?
- What do I want my inner dialogue to sound like a year from now?

Mirror Work Ritual

Stand in front of a mirror. Look into your own eyes. Say something kind, honest, and liberating.

Begin with:

"Even if I don't fully believe it yet, I am learning to love and honor myself."

Do this daily for 30 days. Notice the discomfort, then the shift.

Collective Circle Prompts

For group reflection, community discussions, or shared healing circles:

- What voice of oppression do we share — and how do we challenge it together?
- How has internalized oppression shaped our relationships?
- What new language can we practice as a group to uplift one another?
- How can we hold each other accountable to speak with dignity — to ourselves and each other?

The Liberation Accountability Map

A monthly check-in chart. Rate yourself from 1 (not yet) to 5 (consistently):

Practice	Rating (1–5)
I notice my inner dialogue regularly	
I challenge self-critical thoughts	
I speak to myself with dignity	
I share my healing journey with others	
I integrate new truths into daily life	

Create Your Liberation Language Bank
Start a running list of Liberating Statements you can return to when the inner critic speaks up.
Examples:
- "I don't owe anyone perfection to be worthy."
- "This mistake doesn't erase my progress."
- "I am allowed to take up space and to need care."
- "They tried to shrink me. I'm expanding anyway."

Add to it weekly. Make it yours.

Appendices

Appendix A: Expanded Reflections

Chapter 1: Listening for the Voice Inside — Beyond People, Into Systems

1. What is the voice inside me usually saying when I feel afraid, ashamed, or unsure of myself?
2. When did this voice first begin to speak? Was it tied to a particular event, relationship, or environment?
3. Whose voice does it resemble—someone in your life or a broader social message?
4. How have race, gender, class, ability, or other identities shaped this voice?
5. What has this voice protected you from, and what has it cost you?
6. What would you say to someone you love who heard a voice like this inside themselves?

Chapter 3: Tracking the Impact of Microaggressions

1. Recall a recent microaggression. What happened, and how did it make you feel?
2. What was your internal dialogue in that moment?
3. What part of your body responded to it?
4. How have these small, repeated experiences shaped your self-belief over time?
5. What stories have been reinforced by these moments?
6. What would it sound like to respond to those stories with truth and compassion?

Chapter 4: Naming — and Now What?

1. What recurring inner narratives have I noticed?
2. Where did they come from? Who or what shaped them?
3. How do they influence my behavior and self-worth today?
4. What would it look like to externalize this narrative — write it down or speak it aloud?
5. What's one small new sentence I'm ready to try instead?
6. What kind of person would believe this new sentence — and am I ready to become them?

Chapter 5: Seeing Through the Distortion

1. What do I believe about myself that may have been distorted by past experiences?
2. What systems contributed to this distortion?
3. What has this distorted mirror made me do — or stop doing?
4. What would I see if I looked at myself through a lens of truth and compassion?
5. What moments have I glimpsed my true self — and how can I return to that vision?

Chapter 6: Where Have You Gone Silent?

1. What parts of myself have I hidden to be accepted or safe?
2. Where do I still silence my truth — at work, in relationships, in my own thoughts?
3. What survival strategies do I use? (People-pleasing, over-apologizing, never resting, staying neutral)
4. What have these strategies protected me from — and what have they cost me?
5. What would freedom look like in my daily life — in speech, movement, emotion, expression?
6. What is one small act of liberation I could try this week?

Chapter 7: What If Your Healing Is the Revolution?

1. What forms of healing have I been made to feel guilty or unworthy of?
2. What systems have made healing feel selfish, weak, or indulgent?
3. How do I practice healing in quiet ways — and why is that powerful?
4. What is one act of healing I can do today as a form of resistance?
5. What would it mean to stop earning my worth and start embodying it?

Chapter 8: Practicing a New Voice

1. What's the most dominant inner sentence I'm ready to replace?
2. What sentence would feel like liberation to say instead?
3. How does my body respond to this new sentence?
4. What emotions arise when I try to speak this truth?
5. What's one daily ritual I can create to help anchor this new voice — breath, mirror work, journaling, posture?

Chapter 9: Listening in Real Time

1. When is my inner critic most active — and how do I usually respond?
2. What would it look like to pause and name the voice as it's happening?
3. Can I use breath, grounding, or movement to interrupt the automatic script?
4. What would a compassionate response sound like — even in the middle of noise, conflict, or pressure?
5. What's one real-life moment this week I can practice real-time awareness?

Chapter 10: Practicing Disruption — Without Violence, Without Shame

1. What's one inner belief I'm ready to interrupt?
2. What does my body feel like when that belief takes over?
3. How can I disrupt it — with words, breath, posture, or presence?
4. What would it sound like to speak to myself as a protector, not a punisher?
5. What does gentle, grounded disruption look like in my life?

Chapter 11: Choosing Your New Language

1. What's one sentence I want to believe about myself?
2. What's keeping me from fully believing it?
3. How can I begin to say it anyway — as a practice, not a performance?

4. What would I say to someone I love if they were trying to believe the same sentence?
5. How can I treat this sentence like a seed — not a slogan?

Chapter 12: Practicing Until It Becomes Your Voice

1. How do I treat myself when I forget the new sentence?
2. Can I let repetition become a ritual — not a punishment?
3. What's one small practice I can do each day to anchor this voice? (e.g., breath, movement, mantra)
4. What's shifting in me as I repeat this truth?
5. What would fluency in self-worth look and sound like in my life?

Chapter 13: Taking Up Space Without Asking Permission

1. In what ways do I still shrink, apologize, or self-edit?
2. What would it look like to take up just a little more space — in my words, presence, breath, or posture?
3. What part of me still believes shrinking is safer?
4. What's one space this week where I can practice taking up more room?
5. Can I affirm: I am allowed to be here — fully, unapologetically, and whole?

Chapter 14: Who Are You Healing With?

1. Who makes room for my truth, my wholeness, my becoming?
2. Who do I feel I need to shrink around — and why?
3. What kind of circle am I longing for?
4. How can I co-create healing community, even if I start with just one person?
5. What would it mean to let myself be supported, seen, and softened in the presence of others?

Chapter 15: What Are You Passing On?

1. What have I inherited that I'm ready to release?
2. What do I want to model — in how I speak, rest, parent, teach, or lead?
3. Who is learning from me, even silently?

4. What is one belief I want the next generation to **not** have to carry?
5. What does it look like to model freedom — not perfection?

Chapter 16: How Are You Changing the World Without Even Knowing It?

1. What am I doing differently today that I wasn't doing before?
2. Who might already be feeling the ripple of my healing?
3. What would it mean to believe that my healing is a contribution to collective change?
4. What would it feel like to live as if I belong — fully?
5. What is the story I want my life to tell now?

Appendix B — The Liberation Toolkit

A Companion for Practice, Reflection, and Community Building

This toolkit is designed to help readers apply everything they've just experienced — making the transformation practical, personal, and shareable. It also equips clinicians, educators, group facilitators, and parents to use the content in a broader healing context.

SECTION 1: Inner Dialogue Journaling Prompts

Use these prompts to deepen self-awareness and integrate new narratives.

- What is one sentence I've carried that does not belong to me?
- Whose voice do I hear when I feel afraid or ashamed?
- What do I tend to believe about myself that I'm now ready to question?
- What parts of me have I silenced to stay safe or accepted?
- What does it feel like to take up more space — emotionally, physically, spiritually?
- What would I say to a child or younger version of me who believed they were not enough?
- What does liberation look like in my daily life?

SECTION 2: Daily Self-Affirming Statements for the Liberated Self

Speak aloud. Write them. Whisper them. Repeat them until they feel like home.

- I am worthy without condition.
- My rest is revolutionary.
- I do not need to perform to be valuable.
- I am allowed to take up space.
- My presence is a gift.
- I speak to myself with love, not fear.
- I am breaking patterns, not betraying people.
- Healing is my birthright.
- I am allowed to grow beyond survival.
- I am becoming fluent in self-worth.

SECTION 3: Circle Prompts for Community Use

Use these to start healing conversations with trusted circles or in group work.

1. What messages did you inherit that no longer serve you?
2. What part of yourself have you hidden to be accepted?
3. What does your inner dialogue sound like when you are struggling?
4. What would your inner dialogue sound like if it were rooted in love?
5. What does resistance look like for you?
6. How are you modeling healing for others — intentionally or not?
7. Who would benefit from hearing your truth?

SECTION 4: Mini Practice Guide — The Four Steps of Inner Liberation

1. Awareness
2. Notice the voice. Pause. Breathe.
3. Ask: Whose voice is this? Do I want to keep believing it?
4. Disruption
5. Interrupt the thought with kindness, not aggression.
6. Ask: Is that true? Says who? Is there another way to see this?
7. Replacement
8. Speak a new sentence rooted in truth and dignity.
9. Example: I am not a problem. I am a person in progress.
10. Repetition
11. Practice it daily. Make it a rhythm, not a test.
12. Healing is a muscle. Use it with gentleness and persistence.

SECTION 5: Recommended Readings and Resources

Books

- Sister Outsider by Audre Lorde
- The Body Is Not an Apology by Sonya Renee Taylor
- All About Love by bell hooks
- My Grandmother's Hands by Resmaa Menakem
- The Power of Now by Eckhart Tolle
- The Four Agreements by Don Miguel Ruiz

Practices
- Breath awareness
- Mirror work
- Daily self-talk audits
- Rest as ritual
- Intentional stillness

Community Resources
- Local healing circles or affinity groups
- Trauma-informed coaches or therapists
- Justice-rooted social communities
- Collective care networks (mutual aid, grief groups, accountability circles)

Scientific References

Chapter 1: The Oppressor's Voice in Our Heads
- Fanon, F. (1952). Black Skin, White Masks. Grove Press.
- Freire, P. (1970). Pedagogy of the Oppressed. Continuum.
- Memmi, A. (1965). The Colonizer and the Colonized. Beacon Press.

Chapter 2: Systems That Shape Our Souls
- Crenshaw, K. (1989). Demarginalizing the intersection of race and sex. University of Chicago Legal Forum.
- Sue, D. W., Capodilupo, C. M., et al. (2007). Racial microaggressions in everyday life. American Psychologist, 62(4), 271–286.
- Jones, C. P. (2000). Levels of racism: A theoretic framework and a gardener's tale. American Journal of Public Health, 90(8), 1212–1215.

Chapter 3: From Microaggressions to Mental Imprisonment
- Williams, D. R., & Mohammed, S. A. (2009). Discrimination and racial disparities in health. Journal of Behavioral Medicine, 32(1), 20–47.
- Pierce, C. M. (1974). Psychiatric problems of the Black minority. In American Handbook of Psychiatry (Vol. 2).
- Nadal, K. L. (2018). Microaggressions and Traumatic Stress: Theory, Research, and Clinical Treatment. APA.

Chapter 4: Naming the Inner Narratives
- Beck, A. T. (1967). Depression: Clinical, Experimental, and Theoretical Aspects. University of Pennsylvania Press.
- Young, I. M. (1990). Justice and the Politics of Difference. Princeton University Press.
- Steele, C. M. (1997). A threat in the air: How stereotypes shape intellectual identity and performance. American Psychologist, 52(6), 613–629.

Chapter 5: The Mirror Is Distorted

- Cooley, C. H. (1902). Human Nature and the Social Order. Scribner's.
- Goffman, E. (1959). The Presentation of Self in Everyday Life. Anchor Books.
- Erikson, E. H. (1950). Childhood and Society. Norton.

Chapter 6: When Silence Becomes a Survival Strategy

- Hooks, B. (1989). Talking Back: Thinking Feminist, Thinking Black. South End Press.
- APA (2017). Stress in America: The State of Our Nation. American Psychological Association.
- Tatum, B. D. (1997). Why Are All the Black Kids Sitting Together in the Cafeteria? Basic Books.

Chapter 7: Healing Is Resistance

- Lorde, A. (1984). Sister Outsider: Essays and Speeches. Crossing Press.
- Ginwright, S. (2018). The Future of Healing: Shifting from Trauma Informed Care to Healing Centered Engagement. Medium.
- Prilleltensky, I. (2008). The role of power in wellness, oppression, and liberation. The Counseling Psychologist, 36(2), 116–135.

Chapter 8: A Language of Liberation

- Lakoff, G., & Johnson, M. (1980). Metaphors We Live By. University of Chicago Press.
- Brown, B. (2012). Daring Greatly. Gotham Books.
- Ellis, A. (1994). Reason and emotion in psychotherapy. Revised and Updated Edition.

Chapter 9: Awareness: Hearing the Voice You've Been Ignoring

- Kabat-Zinn, J. (1990). Full Catastrophe Living. Delacorte.
- Segal, Z. V., Williams, J. M. G., & Teasdale, J. D. (2002). Mindfulness-Based Cognitive Therapy for Depression. Guilford Press.
- Siegel, D. J. (2007). The Mindful Brain. W. W. Norton.

Chapter 10: Disruption: Interrupting the Inner Oppressor

- Linehan, M. M. (1993). Cognitive-Behavioral Treatment of Borderline Personality Disorder. Guilford Press.
- Prochaska, J. O., & DiClemente, C. C. (1983). Stages and processes of self-change. Journal of Consulting and Clinical Psychology, 51(3), 390.
- Resmaa Menakem (2017). My Grandmother's Hands. Central Recovery Press.

Chapter 11: Replacement: Planting Seeds of Self-Liberation

- Deci, E. L., & Ryan, R. M. (2000). The "what" and "why" of goal pursuits. Psychological Inquiry, 11(4), 227–268.
- Neff, K. D. (2003). Self-compassion: An alternative conceptualization of a healthy attitude toward oneself. Self and Identity, 2(2), 85–101.
- Seligman, M. E. P. (2002). Authentic Happiness. Free Press.

Chapter 12: Repetition: Becoming Fluent in Self-Worth

- Hebb, D. O. (1949). The Organization of Behavior. Wiley.
- Duhigg, C. (2012). The Power of Habit. Random House.
- Fosha, D. (2000). The Transforming Power of Affect. Basic Books.

Chapter 13: Reclaiming Space and Voice

- Freire, P. (1998). Pedagogy of Freedom: Ethics, Democracy, and Civic Courage. Rowman & Littlefield.
- Delgado, R., & Stefancic, J. (2017). Critical Race Theory: An Introduction. NYU Press.
- Fanon, F. (1963). The Wretched of the Earth. Grove Press.

Chapter 14: Circles of Healing

- Pranis, K. (2005). The Little Book of Circle Processes. Good Books.
- Zimmerman, J., & Coyle, V. (1996). The Way of Council. Bramble Books.
- hooks, bell. (2000). All About Love: New Visions. William Morrow.

Chapter 15: Parenting, Mentoring, and Modeling New Narratives

- Siegel, D. J., & Bryson, T. P. (2011). The Whole-Brain Child. Delacorte.
- Ginsburg, K. R., & Jablow, M. M. (2006). Building Resilience in Children and Teens. American Academy of Pediatrics.
- Garbarino, J. (1999). Lost Boys: Why Our Sons Turn Violent and How We Can Save Them. Free Press.

Chapter 16: Liberation Is Contagious

- Christakis, N. A., & Fowler, J. H. (2009). Connected: The Surprising Power of Our Social Networks. Little, Brown Spark.
- Miller, J. B. (1991). The Healing Connection. Beacon Press.
- Kendi, I. X. (2019). How to Be an Antiracist. One World.

More from SWEET Institute Publishing

At SWEET Institute Publishing, we believe books can be more than information—they can be portals for healing, insight, and change. They can transform.

Every title we publish is a step toward personal and collective liberation, grounded in science, lived experience, and the deep remembering of who we are beneath conditioning.

If Rewriting the Script spoke to you, you're not alone. You are now part of a growing global community of readers, clinicians, social workers, advocates, educators, and everyday change-makers who are choosing to live and lead from a place of truth, freedom, and compassion.

Here are a few other titles from our catalog that continue this work of healing and transformation:

Before Anything Else, Validate
By Mardoche Sidor, MD & Karen Dubin, PhD, LCSW
A paradigm-shifting book that reveals how validation is the foundation of healing, safety, and transformation—in therapy, teams, families, and within ourselves.
Learn the simple, profound art of validation—how it heals, disarms conflict, and rebuilds connection across relationships, systems, and cultures. A must-read for clinicians, caregivers, and leaders alike.

The Clinician's Mirror: A Story of Projection, Self-Discovery, and Healing
By the SWEET Institute Faculty
A powerful narrative-driven exploration of how our internal dynamics as helpers shape the care we give—and how to turn that mirror into a tool for healing ourselves and others.

The Courage to Care: Stories of Healing, Hope, and the Power of Social Work
Edited by Karen Dubin, PhD, LCSW & Mardoche Sidor, MD

50+ social workers share their journeys of becoming, being, and transforming through the profession. A book about legacy, truth-telling, and the radical act of showing up with care.

The Secret Is in Remembering: Why We Suffer, Why We Forget, and How to Return to Who We Are
By SWEET Institute Publishing
A spiritual and scientific exploration of how we forget our inner truth—and how to gently remember, restore, and reclaim the self we were before fear took hold.

Remembering: The Journey Back to the Preconditioned Self
By SWEET Institute Publishing
This poetic and psychological guide walks readers step-by-step through the return to the unconditioned self—free from inherited scripts, shame, and societal masks.

Transforming Team Relationships from the Inside Out: The SWEET Healing Circle for Agencies
By SWEET Institute Publishing
An organizational guide to healing team culture through inner transformation, shared accountability, and real-time connection practices. Designed for agencies ready to lead with humanity.

Join the Movement

SWEET Institute Publishing exists to amplify books that challenge the status quo, illuminate new paths, and help people live from a place of wisdom and authenticity. It creates books for those ready to live, lead, and heal from the inside out.

If this book made a difference for you, share it.
If it gave you language, insight, or strength, pass it on.
Let's keep rewriting the script—together.

About the Authors

Mardoche Sidor, MD

Dr. Sidor is a Harvard- and Columbia-trained, quadruple board-certified psychiatrist in General Psychiatry, Child and Adolescent Psychiatry, Addiction Psychiatry, and Forensic Psychiatry. He is also trained in Public and Community Psychiatry and Geriatric Psychiatry. Formerly an Assistant Clinical Professor of Psychiatry at Columbia University, Dr. Sidor currently serves as Medical Director at Urban Pathways and is a candidate at the Columbia University Center for Psychoanalytic Training and Research. He is the Founder of the SWEET Institute, where he leads a global movement for experiential learning, clinician healing, and mental health transformation from the inside out.

Karen Dubin, PhD, LCSW

Dr. Dubin is a social worker, educator, and writer with decades of experience in trauma recovery, narrative therapy, and clinician development. She is the co-founder and Chief Operating Officer at the SWEET Institute, where she co-leads programs that center clinician healing, radical validation, and real-world application of theory. Her work focuses on rehumanizing the mental health field by bringing dignity, presence, and curiosity into every layer of care.

Adaiah Lassalle, LCSW

Adaiah Lassalle is a licensed clinical social worker, healing-centered practitioner, and advocate for racial and social justice. A proud Black woman and daughter of Caribbean lineage, Adaiah brings deep personal and professional insight into the lived experiences of internalized oppression. Her work focuses on intergenerational healing, trauma-informed care, and rewriting inherited narratives. She facilitates healing spaces for individuals and communities to reclaim their voice, worth, and joy.

Together, these authors bring lived experience, clinical wisdom, and a shared commitment to healing inner narratives shaped by systems of harm. Rewriting the Script is more than a book—it is their collective offering to a world ready to live free.

.

www.ingramcontent.com/pod-product-compliance
Lightning Source LLC
Chambersburg PA
CBHW040845120626
46547CB00001B/26